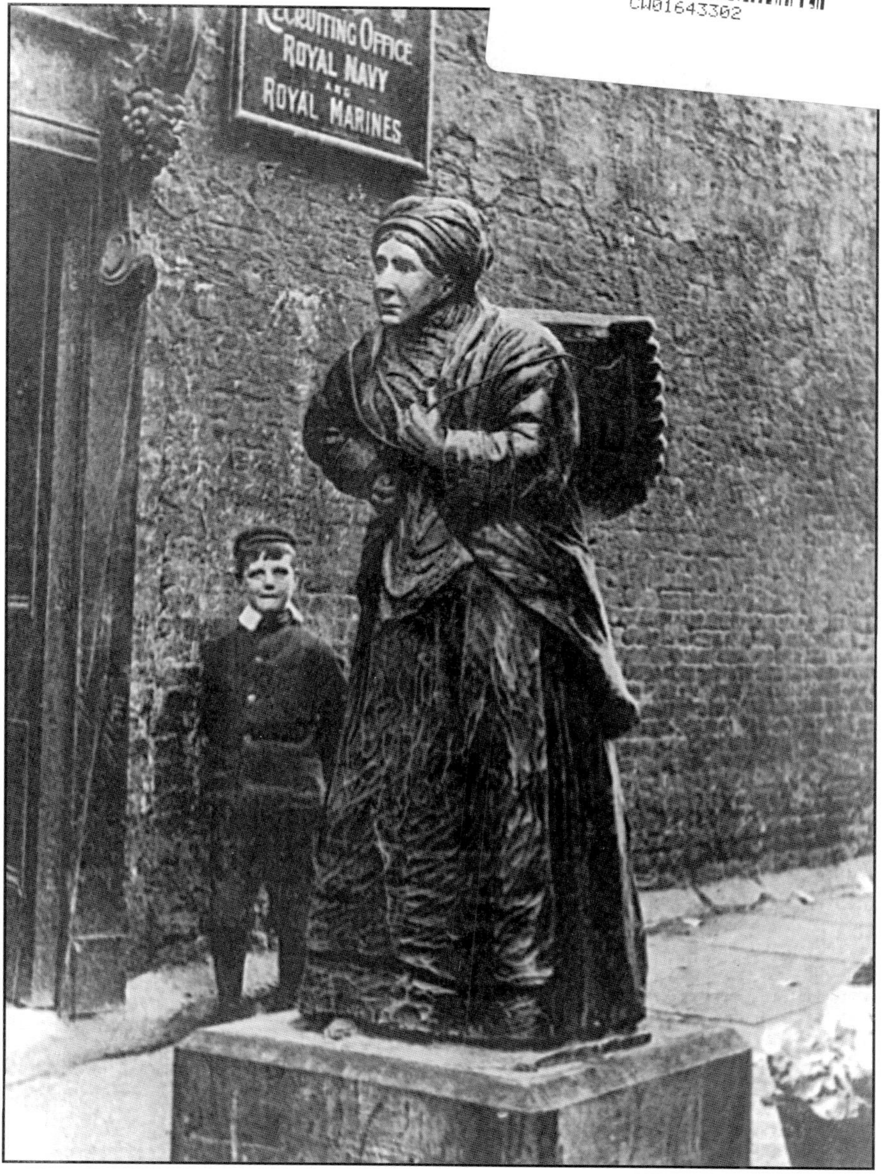
RECRUITING OFFICE
ROYAL NAVY
AND
ROYAL MARINES

THE WOODEN DOLLY

The story of the North Shields Wooden Dolly

Edited by Keith Armstrong

Design & new photographs
by Peter Dixon

Published by North Tyneside Libraries, Central Library,
Northumberland Square, North Shields, Tyne & Wear NE30 1QU,
Telephone 258 2811
in association with Northern Voices.

Printed by C.V.N. Print, Charles Newton Building, Commercial Road,
South Shields, Tyne & Wear NE33 5SH.
Telephone 455 3703.

ISBN 0 906529 14 X

INTRODUCTION

This book, commissioned from the 'Northern Voices' community publishing project by North Tyneside Libraries, tells the story of the legendary North Shields Wooden Dolly. It offers an historical background to what amounts now to six Wooden Dollies, re-prints original newspaper-cuttings and documents, and reproduces all of the available historical photographs on the subject, supplemented by present-day photos.

There are various accounts of the Wooden Dollies. Our introductory history of each Dolly is as accurate as possible.

An additional feature is a selection of poems and stories by Tyneside people especially written for the book with the encouragement of the Editor.

Keith Armstrong,
Editor.

BIOGRAPHY

KEITH ARMSTRONG is a poet and community publisher who lives in Whitley Bay. A qualified librarian, he has organised community festivals in Shiremoor and Earsdon over the years and has been responsible for establishing many writing and publishing enterprises locally, including 'Strong Words' and 'Northern Voices', which is based in North Shields.

He has recently edited a selection of poems on shipyard life by 'Ripyard Cuddling', also published by North Tyneside Libraries, and a book on the Durham Miners' Gala. He has read his own poems at events all over Britain, in Russia, Iceland (during the Cod War), Germany, Holland, the European Parliament in Strasbourg, and several other countries.

THE DOLLY STORY

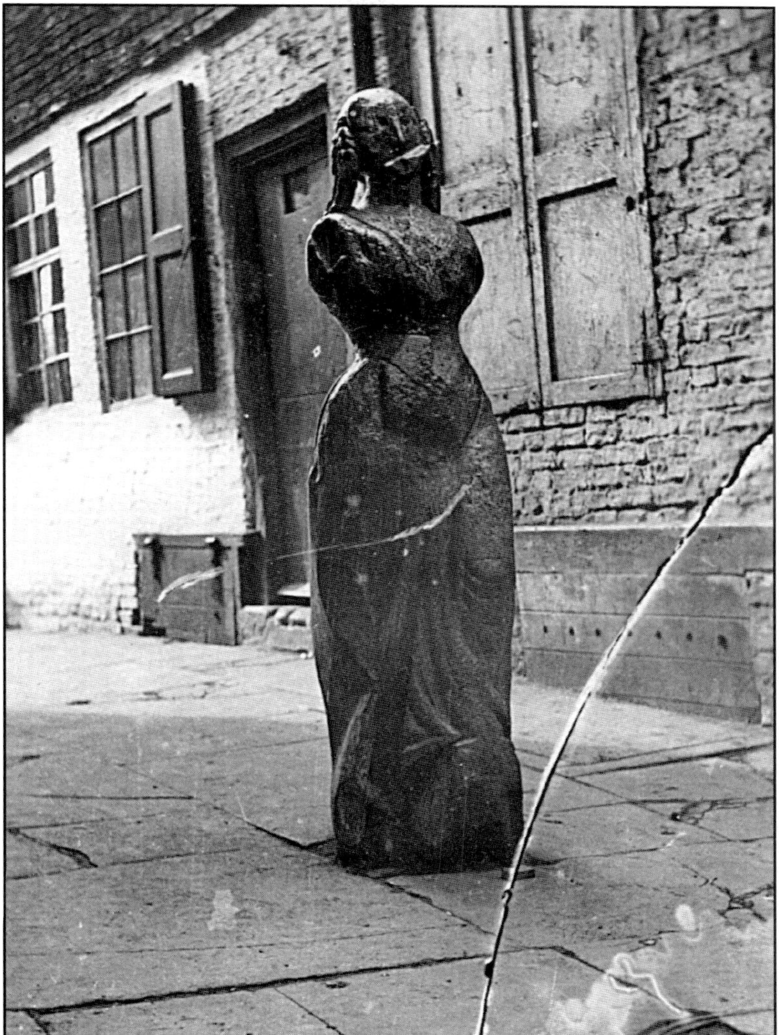

Wooden Dolly 3

DOLLY, OUR DOLLY

There stood a Wooden Dolly upon a Northern quay,
but not a bairn that played around could take her on her knee,
O, not a bairn could dangle her, nor carry her to bed -
So there the Wooden Dolly stood, be sun or storm o'erhead:
The plaything of the wind and rain, as cheery as could be,
The Wooden Dolly stood and smiled upon a Northern quay.

There stood a Wooden Dolly, upon a Northern quay,
the love of every sailor lad a-coming home from sea,
and every jolly sailor lad would pare a little chip,
because it was a lucky thing to take aboard his ship,
they chipped and pared, and nicked and notched,
   until no more was she!
and that's another standing now upon a Northern quay.

Queenie Scott-Roper
('Shields Hustler', Autumn 1916)

THE ORIGINAL WOODEN DOLLY, c.1814-1850

The original Wooden Dolly was a figurehead on a collier brig called the 'Alexander & Margaret' - named after its owner, Alexander Bartleman, a North Shields shipbuilder, and his wife Margaret. It was positioned in the front garden of their house at 23 Front Street, Tynemouth in memory of Bartleman's son, David, Captain of the brig, who was mortally wounded off Yarmouth in 1781 defending his ship against the infamous Captain William Fall in the 'Fearnought'. Out-gunned and out-manned, David Bartleman resisted three attacks from the 'Fearnought', but, after the fourth, had to 'strike his colours', because he was badly wounded. The brig put into Yarmouth where he died and was buried.

The Wooden Dolly was moved in 1814 to her position on the Custom House Quay, Low Street, North Shields where she served as a barrier to vehicles backing down the Quay and thereby causing a nuisance to people living and working nearby.

The original Dolly seems to have been a comely creature. Paul Trumpeter, local historian, was evidently seduced by her charms when he described her as 'no slim, simpering, Goddess-looking creature, but a bluff, saucy, hearty-looking hussey, with a full flaunting petticoat something in the style of good Queen Bess.'

But such charms did not save her from the indignity of having warps turned round her ankles to draw spars and baulks up the Quay. Needless to say such treatment hastened her demise. After being chipped and pared by seamen and the local street urchins she was in a sad state when on one fateful day a party of drunks stopped to abuse her and finally tore her from the ground. The next morning she was found with a broken neck, the head being used to prop up the decapitated body.

THE SECOND WOODEN DOLLY, c.1850-1864

The original Dolly's replacement was placed on the same site on the quay by a Mr. Hare, a sailmaker. It is believed that the second Dolly was also a figurehead, although nothing is known of its origin.

THE THIRD WOODEN DOLLY, 1864-1901

More is known of Dolly number three, who enjoyed a relatively long life. She was formally the figurehead of the barque 'Expert', belonging to Peter and John Stephenson. In 1864, while the vessel was being repaired by chandlers, Harcus & Stroud, the figurehead was removed to serve as the third Wooden Dolly. William Street recorded that, on 23rd June 1864, the foundation stone of the Low Lights Dock was laid, and was supposed to bring a new prosperity to North Shields. It was considered an appropriate time to remove the old Dolly and replace it with a new and more beautiful figure. This new 'Wooden Lady' was placed in position without ceremony by Mr. John Larkus and Mr. James Pringle on the evening of 22nd June 1864. But the figure had not been in position long before it was subjected to the same indignities as its predecessors. The chipping and hacking continued until at one stage major surgery was required to remodel poor Dolly's nose. The delicate operation was entrusted to Robert Pow, a well-known blacksmith in Liddell Street, who skilfully inserted an iron nose which resisted all further attacks, until her demise at the turn of the century.

After drilling a hole in a coin, sailors on the Quayside used to nail it into the third Wooden Dolly for good luck.

Nearly seventy years after her replacement, the third Dolly resurfaced in the possession of a Mr. Seery, a Newcastle antique dealer, who purchased her from a fisherman's widow, and after being on display in his antique rooms for many years, she was finally bought by a Dane and is believed to form part of a collection in a Denmark museum.

Mr. Seery observed that 'she had not a flake of paint on her - her nose was missing and she appeared quite a formidable sight.'

THE FOURTH WOODEN DOLLY, 1902-1957

A fourth Wooden Dolly was carved by May Spence of North Shields at the bequest of her late reverend father Alderman John Foster Spence, on condition that it was to be positioned on the same site as the first three Dollies.

The fourth Dolly took the form of a fishwife with a creel on her

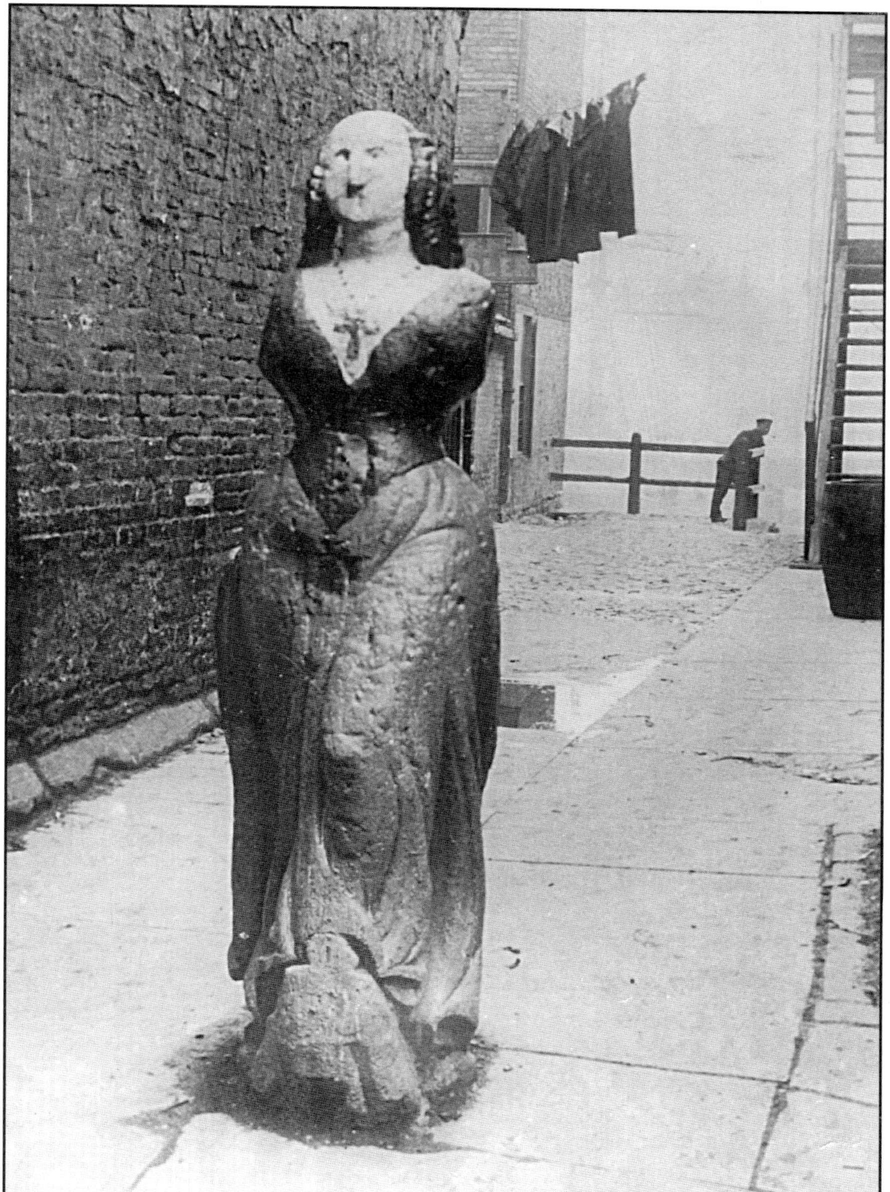

Wooden Dolly 3

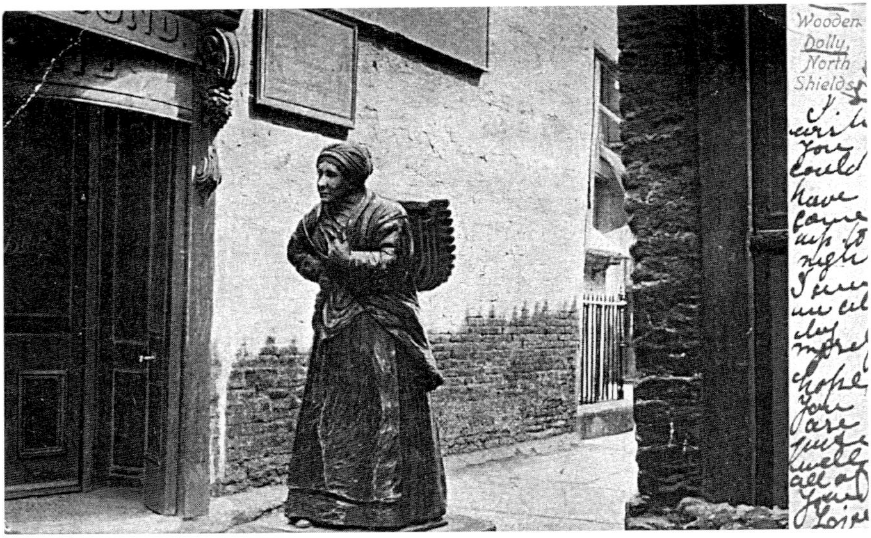

back and stirred up controversy because she was so different to the previous ones

The unveiling of May Spence's Dolly took place on Coronation Day 26th June 1902 at 10.00am.

May Spence's Dolly survived for more than half a century before it too became so mutilated that it had to be replaced.

Her missing right elbow was presented to an hotel in Melbourne, Victoria, Australia. She was found by two lady residents of North Shields lying in a breaker's yard in Whitby, Yorkshire.

THE FIFTH WOODEN DOLLY, 1958 to date

As a tribute to May Spence, the civic authorities decided that the new figure, the product of a fund established by the Mayor of Tynemouth in the 1950s, would be unveiled on the 22nd October, 1958, the day on which she celebrated her hundredth birthday. The remains of the fourth Dolly were taken to the workshops of Robert Thompson Ltd., of Kilburn, Yorkshire, whose craftsmen were to carve the new Dolly. Two small mice, the trademark of Robert Thompson, which signifies 'industry in quiet places', were carved on the new figure. A tradition of 144 years old was broken with the choice of a

THE NEW DOLLY IS UNVEILED

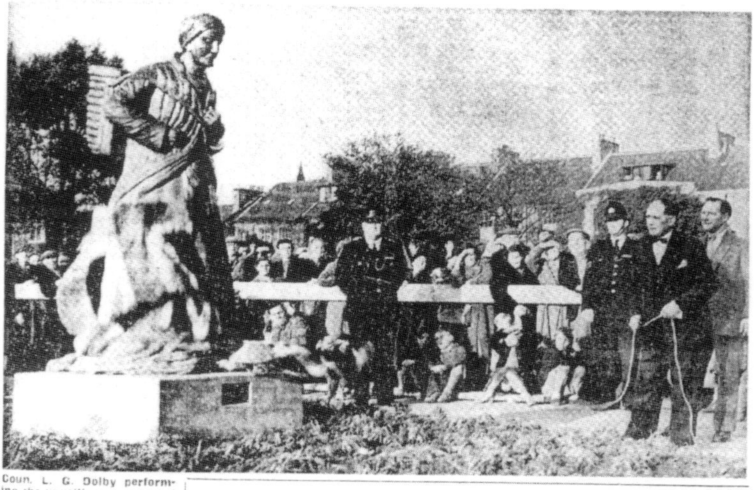

Coun. L. G. Dolby performing the unveiling ceremony of the Wooden Dolly in Northumberland Square, North Shields, yesterday.

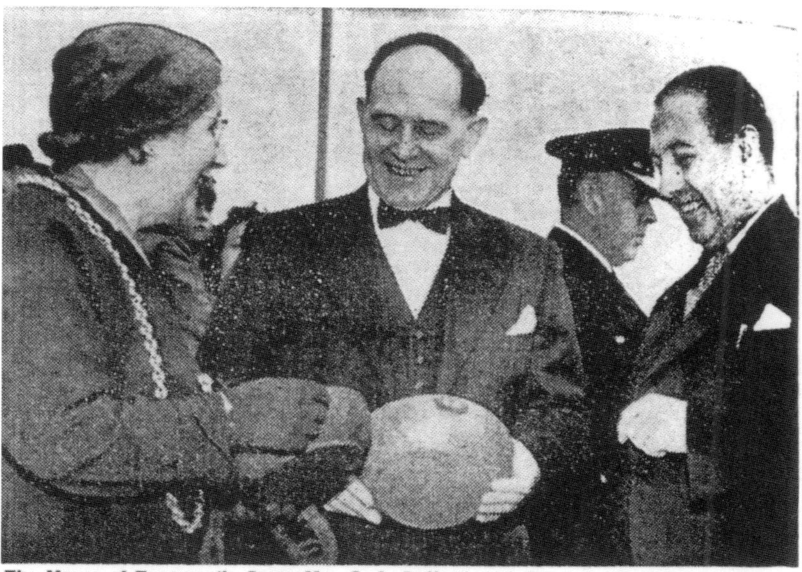

The Mayor of Tynemouth, Coun. Mrs. S. A. Ballard and Coun. L. G. Dolby admiring the carved bowls bearing the mouse insignia presented to them by Mr. Arthur Dickinson, editor of The Evening News, after the unveiling ceremony.

site for the fifth Dolly. She now enjoys a place in the heart of Northumberland Square.

Carved in mahogany, after thirty years of weathering, restoration work was carried out on her in 1986.

THE SIXTH WOODEN DOLLY, 1992 to date

A new Wooden Dolly, a copy of the third, now stands outside the Prince of Wales, re-opened on 20th October 1992, on Custom House Quay, the original site of the third Dolly.

Sculpted out of a single block of oak costing £5,000, the sixth Dolly weighs one and a half tons.

The Prince of Wales was built originally in 1674 and rebuilt in 1927. It was at one time known as 'The Wooden Dolly'.

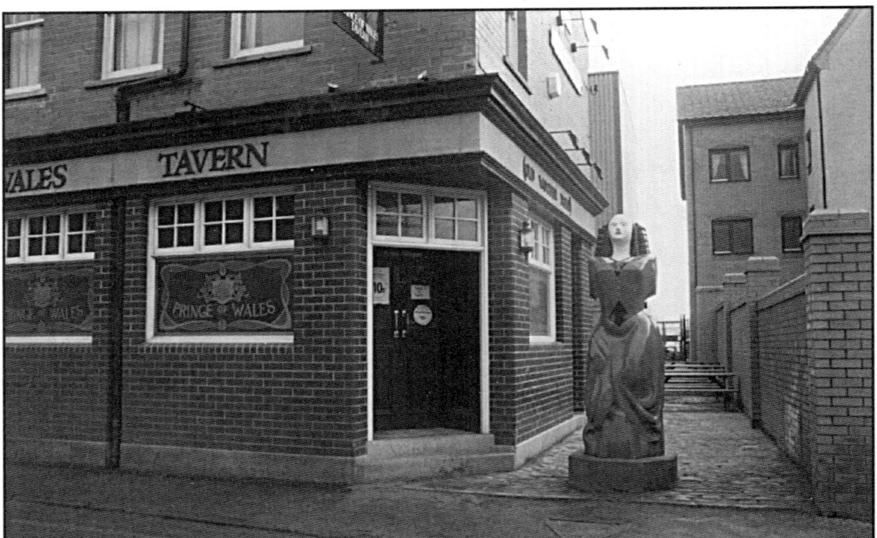

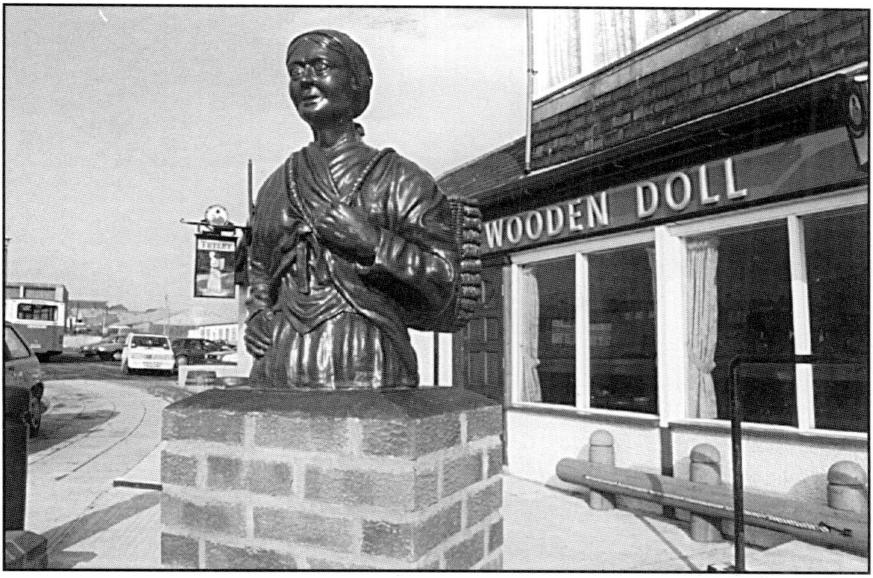

N.B. A Dolly on the lines of a Cullercoats fish-wife can be seen outside the Wooden Doll public house. It was sculpted by Laurence Gardner, 1992-3, and is moulded in clay and cast in sculptural plaster.

(The editor wishes to thank David Craven, author of 'The Mystery of the Wooden Dollies'; Brian Hunter, author of an article in 'Northern Life'; and local historian Stephen Moore for help with source material.)

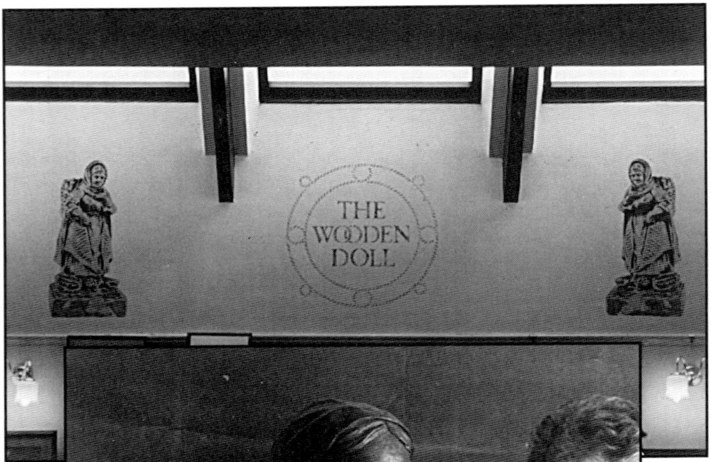

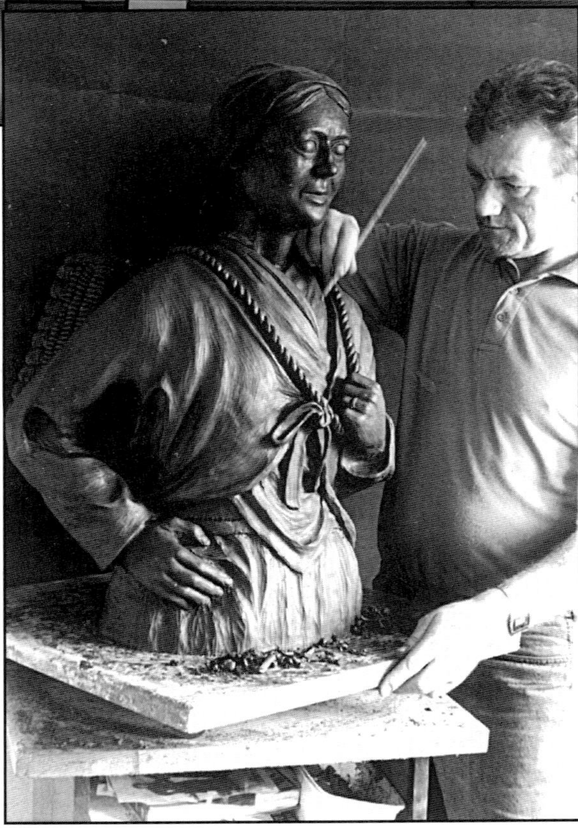

Sculptor Laurence Gardner at work
Above: interior of 'The Wooden Doll' pub

DOLLY POEMS & STORIES

Writing by local people

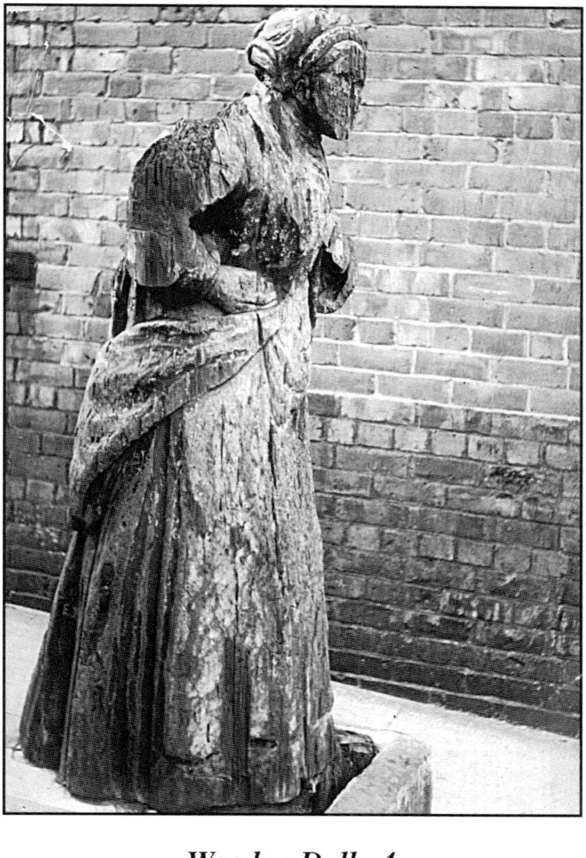

Wooden Dolly 4
Photo by E. Walton

THE WOODEN DOLLY

For many years she stood upon the Fish Quay
A problematic symbol of the past
The figurehead of some forgotten trader
She had travelled many miles before the mast.

And everyone paid homage to the lady
She was worshipped by the seamen's brotherhood
Amazing when you think that she was only
An ordinary Dolly made of wood.

They came from every corner of the nation
Like pilgrims on their journey to a shrine
And they gathered there in silent acclamation
Round that Dolly on the North side of the Tyne.

Now the Wooden Doll was famous but unhappy
She was mugged by cruel vandals through the years
They chipped large lumps of wood from off her person
And they carried them away for souvenirs.

As a consequence she started getting thinner
Till the day arrived that everyone had feared
The vandals had removed their final plunder
And the poor old Wooden Doll had disappeared.

The 'Canny folk of Shields' were broken hearted
When they heard about the famous Doll's demise
So they had a 'Whip around' to buy another
On the Quay another Dolly would arise.

A brand new Doll was placed upon the Quayside
On the very spot where once had stood the first
But the 'Canny folk of Shields' had backed a loser
For once again the vandals did their worst.

Now fishermen have long been known to linger
At the 'Prince of Wales', a pub beside the Quay
And there outside that pub in all her splendour
Is where they planted Dolly number three.

And there for many years she kept her station
She began her stint in eighteen sixty four
Ravaged by the years and local villains
Till a sister Doll took over at the door.

The Doll no longer stands beside the fish quay
But she's still around if you would care to look
If you climb up Borough Bank and turn to starboard
You will find her in another, safer nook.

And when you come to Shields please pay a visit
To the library that stands beside the Square
If you look across the road behind the railings
You will see a wooden lady standing there.

And she is proof if you should ever need it
That through the years a legend can survive
For the lady standing there in all her glory
Is the North Shields Wooden Dolly number five.

Jack Davitt
(Ripyard Cuddling)

When Herbert Mangle, the Wallsend poet, composed the following, it had been his intention to write *Kubla Khan*, but his sister said, "It's already been done, you fool!"

Denigration

Was Shelley's traveller from an antique land
　　Aghast at Ozymandias and his folly?
So Percy said. But did he ever stand
　　And contemplate our cryptic Wooden Dolly?

Would Keats, quite ardent in poetic duty,
　　Have asked, "What boots this object less than couth?
It fails most surely as a thing of beauty,
　　And so by definition tells no truth."

And would old Wordsworth, had he chanced to pass,
　　Imbued as ever with divine intentions,
Have seen a thing of splendour in the grass,
　　Or merely suffered crowds of apprehensions?

Would even Stratford's Will, prolix with words,
　　Have cooed, "This Doll outshines a summer's day"?
Or would he not have left her to the birds
　　And "Out damn'd spot!" been likelier to say?

Envoy

But art apart, our Dolly's lore belongs
　　In epic mystery? And legends bright?
And esoteric myths, evoking songs
　　That Homer might have sung? Well no, not quite.

Herbert Mangle (1883-1965)

THE WOODEN DOLLY

She stood there all the winter,
    And all the summer too,
Never ate, nor drank, nor slept,
    Not even a word to you,
Though sailors all admired her,
    She was never very jolly,
Because this lady, so well known,
    Was just a Wooden Dolly.

When every skipper came ashore,
    To pay a visit here,
Each one chipped a little piece,
    Just for a souvenir,
They stripped pieces from her apron,
    Her fishing creel, her hair,
Now she's all brand new again,
    In Northumberland Square.

Margaret Johnson

'WOR DOLLY'

Eeh, 'Wor Dolly'
You're a canny lass,
Thy's weathered the storms
And seen ships as they've passed.
What tales you could tell
If you weren't made of wood.
What would you say
If only you could?
Would you recall the seafaring men
Who chipped you to pieces before they went hyem?
Poor old doll, you've had some bashing,
Figurehead on a ship, where the wind gave you a lashing.
In years gone by, you were treated with love
As a lucky charm by sailors with the sea in their blood.
Today 'Wor Dolly' you're standing alone
In the centre of Shields which is now your new home.
People pass by and, maybe, they stare
At a piece of wood sculptured with care.
But do they ever wonder and maybe think
That you 'Wor Doll' have history with a seafaring link?

Margaret Jean Wilcock

THE DOLLIES OF NORTH SHIELDS

From the early 1800s, Low Street has been home
to a series of model women of the silent wooden kind,
set up to serve, as bollard, but abused by some
seamen taking 'lucky chips' with knives.

First to dwell there was a brave and hearty lass 1814
a collier brig she once breasted to
survivor of a battle at sea, privateer infested. mid
Her end came when drunkards broke her neck, alas! 1800s

In place of the first unlucky dame c1850
came another of similar ilk to
set up by a sailmaker, at his will. 1864
Silence shrouds her passing, having no claim to fame.

Proud doll the third, reigned for many years 1864
a sister of those other maritime girls to
popular and well loved by all, 1901
giving name to quay, and pub, and stairs.

1902 produced a different female figure, 1902
a canny fishwife bearing creel upon her back, until
causing quite a stir and a great deal local crack. 1957
Patience was her virtue for five and fifty years.

A replacement fishwife looks down toward the Tyne 1958
from Northumberland Square, her elevated station.
Craftsman Thompson's mice are hidden on her person.
Well preserved against vandals, and the ravages of time.

Another figure-head doll takes stance
brazen, more colourful than her mates;
close by the pub, in renovated state,
on a quayside newly enhanced.

Oct.
20th
1992

If you should visit the Square, or North Shields Custom Quay,
look kindly on these Dollies,
and whether or not you go to sea
avoid past sailors' follies.

Freda Booth

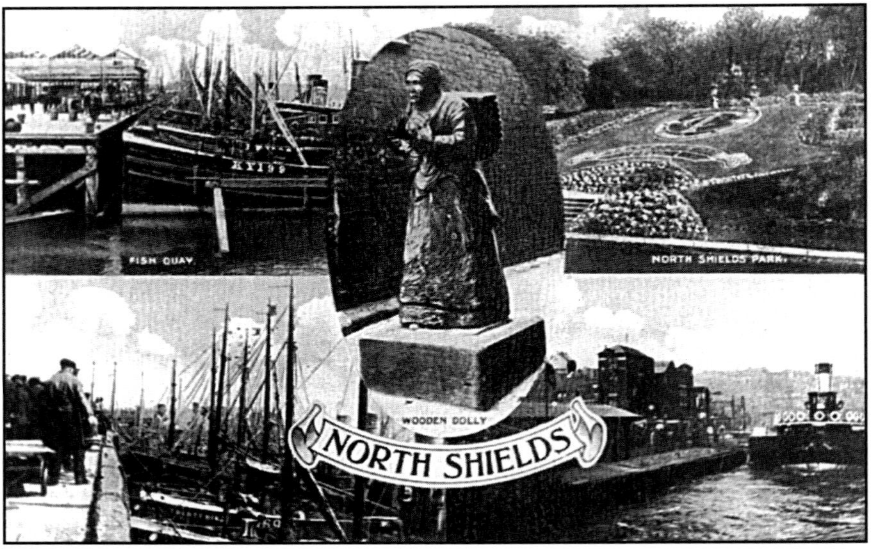

BALLAD OF THE WOODEN DOLLY

(or - The Dolly by the Quay)

(1)
They'd saved her from a wrecker's yard
Upon a distant shore,
And there beside the Custom House,
For many years and more,
They patched her and they painted her
And drank her health, in ale.
- Fine lady from a collier brig
That never more would sail.

Chorus
Aye, silence was her watchword
And so proud of cast was she,
In pickled brine, beside the Tyne,
Down Low Street by the Quay.

(2)
And Sailor lads from foreign parts
Would trim her goodly gown.
- Fine chippings ta'en for Lady Luck
When they were on the town.
In wind and rain she'd not complain,
And children laughed with glee
As up they'd go
On heel and toe
Round Dolly by the Quay.

Chorus

(3)
From ear to ear, they shaved her sheer,
Her nose was spliced in three,
While hidden legs made Dolly pegs
For loved-ones o'er the sea.
They clipped her hip, they chipped her nose;
T'was pitiful to see
How Dolly then was treated
As she lingered by the Quay.

Chorus

(4)
And it came about one midnight clear,
Beneath a sequinned sky,
There staggered from the tavern door
Six drunkards wond'ring why
This lady should be standing there
So near their brawling den,
Upon a night of revelry,
Within a world of men.

Chorus

(5)
Then one whose name is lost in time
Addressed his mates. Sez he,
"Aa canna stand yon gaupin' wife,
What divil's right hez she
Tae hang aroond oor sacred groond?
Noo divvent yous aall opine
'tis time we lads hed done with hor
An' hoyed hor in the Tyne?"

Chorus

(6)
They chaffed her and they gaffed her
And they cut her round the knee;
They buffed her and they cuffed her
As they made with her so free.
They slashed her and they gashed her
And tore strips from her bright gown,
The night those drunken sailors came
To pull poor Dolly down.

Chorus

(7)
But when at length, the break of day
Bathed canny Shields in light,
Some keelmen passin' by the Quay
Came on that awful sight.
- The Wooden Dolly broken down
With severed head as well.
What filled them with compassion
Only loving hearts can tell.

Chorus

(8)
They heaved her up and set her head
Upon her neck once more;
They patched her and they painted
Round the ravaged clothes she wore;
They gave the Doll a grand new nose
And stood her by the Quay
In pickled brine, beside the Tyne
For everyone to see.

Chorus

FINAL VERSE
(9)
Now other Dollies there have been
To take the old girl's place;
And other sailors have been seen
To hack them round the face,
But here's three cheers for our first Doll.
- No Doll so brave as she.

May canny Shieldsfolk ne'er forget
That Dolly by the Quay.

Chorus

Aye, silence was her watchword
And so proud of cast was she,
In pickled brine, beside the Tyne
Down Low Street by the Quay.

Bernard M. Jackson

FIVE WOODEN DOLLIES

ONE - for a brig that fought and was lost,
But carried its colours with pride.
TWO - for another, in tempest tossed,
When many a seaman died.
THREE - for the sails of an elegant barque
That billowed to far distant shores.
FOUR - for the wife who devoted her life
To the fight for the fisherman's cause.
AND FIVE - for the fields
That gave canny Shields
A township that's come to be.
----- Five Dolls,
One by one.
Aye, it wasn't for fun;
T'was the pride o' the town, y' see.

Bernard M. Jackson

GUD LUCK T' SHIELDS

Aw, hadaway man, hadaway,
An' shut yor gob for fairs;
Noo divvent y' knaa thet Dolly theor
(They've getten doon th' chares)
Ez nee jus' theor tee clag th' raa,
A maisor tho' it be,
Se nivvor fash you clivvor heed
'boot Dolly by th' Quay.

Aa knaa whin baith on us wez bairns
An' heor we yewsed t' play,
Thor wez nee Dolly, thor's nee doot,
But noo she's cum t'stay.
Y'see, wor brig lads needs hor luck
Tae roond th' Midden Rocks.
    —A chippin' heor,
    A chippin' theor
T' save 'em fra hard knocks;
Se divvent blather 'boot yon wife
    —Oor seaman aall agree
    'tis guid luck seun mun cum t'Shields
    Fra Dolly by the Quay.

Bernard M. Jackson

IN PRIDE O' PLACE

Tiggy touch-wood,
Dance around,
Young lover's tryst
And sailor's luck:
A chipping for
Black Midden Rocks,
A paring
For the North Sea storm.

Poor old lady, poor old wife,
What tales ye'd tell could we but know,
What tales ye'd tell
Of sailing days
And where the fearsome
North winds blow.

Aye, once she was a figurehead
Afore a gallant collier true,
A brig whose lads were Shieldsmen bred,
No finer men, no braver crew;
For on that luckless final trip
'Twixt Yarmouth and the coaly Tyne,
A privateer, some Dunkirk ship,
Had signalled them to fall in line.
The brig was hopelessly outgunned,
Her sails were rent with shot and ball.
Her young crew fought --- Her captain shunned
Surrender to the pirate's call.
For two long hours fought the brig
Till crew were maimed and mate was dead.
The privateer then took the ship,
But spared the lovely figurehead.

That's how she came,
That's how she came,
That's how she came so strange of form
For

    Tiggy touch-wood,
    Dance around,
    Young lover's tryst
    And sailor's luck:
    A chipping for
    Black Midden Rocks,
    A paring
    For the North Sea storm.

Bernard M. Jackson

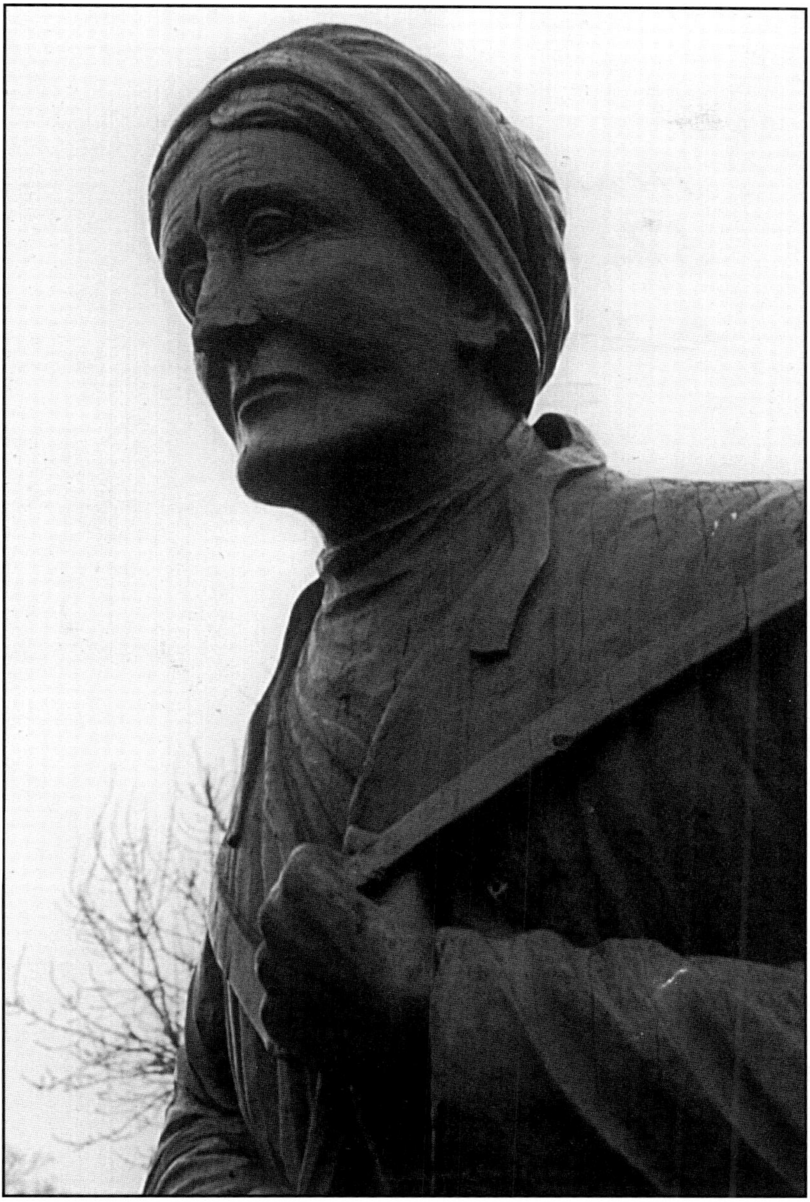

Wooden Dolly 5

It happened like this. Two girls sat on the grass. Let us call one girl Mary, the other Catherine. They were watching the statue in the park. Mary said she'd heard a woman say that it had moved, all the way from the river, right up to here. She said, she'd heard this woman telling another woman and it must be a Miracle. Mary, who went to church every day during Lent spoke as if she knew all there was to know about Miracles.

"They've got them in Ireland," she went on.

"What?"

"Statues that move. Miracle statues."

Catherine looked at the carved figure of the woman with the basket on her back.

"But this isn't a real statue. I mean it's not a Holy one, or anything like that."

"They stand for hours waiting for them to move. Sometimes they cry."

"Who cries?"

"The statues. In Ireland."

And on the strength of this they decided to see if this one would move, or cry, or both.

Catherine looked closely. There weren't any tears. There was bird dirt.

"How long will we have to wait?" she asked, poking a bundle of dead leaves with her shoe. Mary shrugged her shoulders.

"Days, probably."

They waited until four o'clock and the statue didn't move. They waited until ten past four and still, it didn't move. Catherine noticed that Mary seemed to have forgotten all about miracles, she was watching a group of boys racing about; shouting and fighting each other in piles on the ground. Two of the boys jumped on to the seat where an old woman sat throwing bread from a basket. She was surrounded by birds. She wore a blue hat. The boys knocked it over to one side of her head.

"Get your feet off the seat." The woman had a voice thin as paint. "Go on. Get Off." She took off her hat and waved it at them. Mary started to giggle. Catherine looked at her as if unsure how to react. A smile dragged her mouth and she, too, began to laugh, the merest of laughs, an uncertain sort of laugh. It made her look away, up at the trees, down at the ground.

"Stupid old woman" a boy shouted. The others joined him in a slow chant.

"Stu-pid. Stu-pid." It started with a low rumble, the rumble of drums, and rose steadily, scattering the birds from the trees. "Stupid. Stupid."

The woman stood up and hit the nearest boy. She hit him hard and accurately on the nose, right in the middle of it so that blood poured out all over his mouth. She kept on hitting him with such ferocity that her false teeth worked loose and the boy escaped to the shadow of a tree. The others laughed at the old woman's gaping mouth. They laughed at the larval flow of saliva on her chin. The two girls sat, hands up to their mouths, hiding their laughter. They watched as the boys began to pick up their coats. The old woman, whose teeth were hanging between her lips as if she was eating them, shouted something at the boys but it came out muffled and full of spit. She continued to punch.

She was a small woman. Neat as knitting. But she punched like a boxer while the boy with burst nose stood and watched from under a tree. The blood wouldn't stop. All he had was his sleeve to wipe it on. He picked up his coat and moved off, sniffing and coughing.

"Scuse me." a lady said. She looked at the girls. They stopped giggling. She looked at the old woman dancing around kicking and punching at the air; sweat pouring from the sides of her head, pouring faster than the blood from the boy's nose. The park was now empty of boys.

"I said, excuse me." The girls moved to let the lady through but she stood beside them and watched as the last of the boys disappeared, dodging cars across the street. Then she moved to where the old woman pirouetted like a tangled puppet. She raised her hand and at once the old woman stopped, breathless and wet around her mouth where her teeth had been. The dentures lay on the ground, the upper set broken clean in two.

There was a sudden burst of thunder and as suddenly rain dashed at the ground. The girls screeched with a mixture of shock and pleasure, holding their faces up to catch the rain on their tongues. They made fish mouths as they spun. Within minutes they were completely soaked. Then they ran hard along the road to home.

The old woman stood under the tree where the bloodied boy had been. She peered at the grass as if searching for evidence of his injury. She wiped the sweat from her face. Mopped up the tears. She wrapped the broken dentures in a grey handkerchief and pushed them into her pocket.

The newcomer joined her and their shadows met beneath the tree.

Slowly, as one of advanced years might, a figure walked towards the plinth. A basket bent her spine till it was almost double. She hoisted up her skirts clear of the puddles. Mice dodged her steps, hitched a ride on her petticoats. Church bells rang.

It was almost dark when the girls reached home. Their clothes dripped water on the steps of their adjoining houses. Their mothers were not pleased. Their mothers spoke heatedly of coming home late. They ranted about strangers in alleyways. They sent their daughters to bed. The girls forgot about the statue.

Later that evening an old lady sat at the back of a bus. She sat until the driver noticed and asked to see her pass. It was ten-thirty. He moved up the aisle and as he did his face took on a look of confusion. The woman stared at him drunkenly. There was a lopsidedness to her features, a wetness about her mouth. Her hat, a blue woollen one, tilted over her left eye. She growled from low in her throat when he asked if everything was alright. Everything was not alright.

In the paper next day, notice was given of the theft, during the night, of the statue in the park. Notice was also given of the Lord Mayor's reward of one hundred pounds for any information leading to its whereabouts.

Celia Bryce

DOLLY CUTTINGS

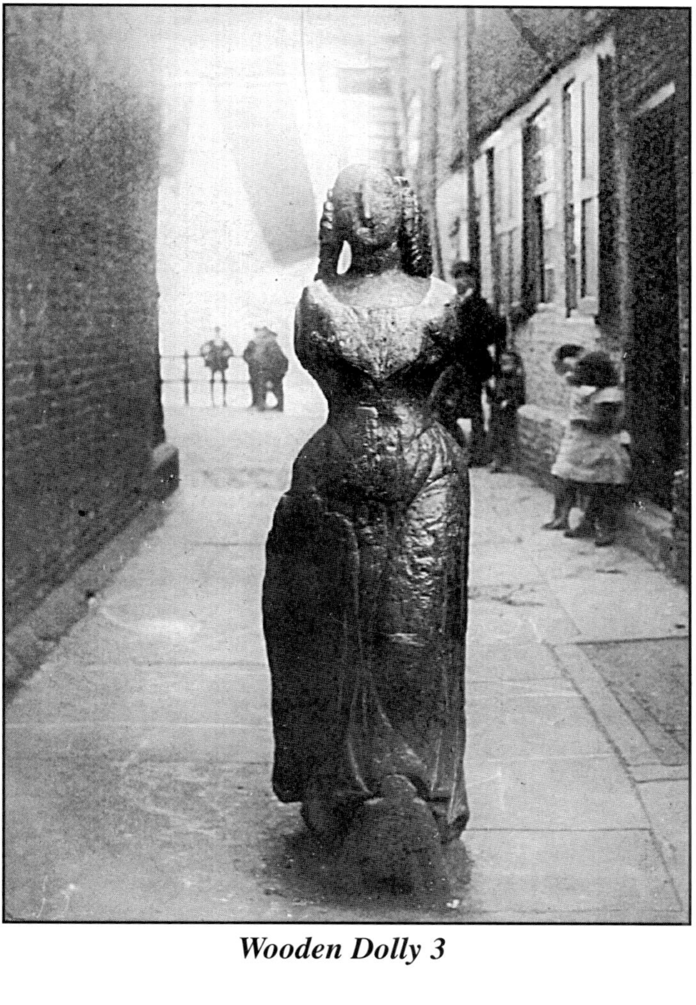

Wooden Dolly 3

OLD NORTH SHIELDS

The history of the Wooden Dolly at North Shields is lost in the shades of antiquity. Its history is so old that when a writer first wrote about it he suggested that the Wooden Dolly had been first set up at North Shields about the year 1814 - some 75 years before he put the tradition into print.

Again, in stating why it was set up the writer says - "I am unable to give the exact date, but about the year 1814, Mr. Alexander Bartleman owned an old Collier Brig that was being put into the docks for repair; and while there, the figure head was taken off and placed where the present Dolly stands". Does the writer wish us to imply a former Dolly stood there?

I do not think so; because he goes on to say - "There were previously posts, or a bar, across the Quay. At the time the figure was placed in position there was a small garden plot on the Custom House Quay, and also trees near it as high as the tops. He also suggests Mr. Bartleman put it there to prevent traffic going on to the Quay and that carts must approach it by another route."

I myself would suggest that the Dolly had been placed in position much earlier than the year 1814 - I suggest it was placed there about the year about the end of 1781 - a time when this country was at war with France, Spain, Holland and the American Colonies.

It is strange that North Shields people - ever fond of writing to the local paper between the years 1800 and 1900 never once in a local paper write about the Wooden Dolly - the reason is that its history goes so far back that the Wooden Dolly has always been a relic that the townspeople have taken it for granted. Later and not many years ago, it is true we have writers telling us of other Dollies being erected on the spot.

I make a bold suggestion that the ship called the 'Alexander and Margaret' was built during the war of 1781 by Mr. Bartleman, a North Shields ship builder - and he built many ships at the time - and that it was called after himself and his wife. So far I have not been able to learn the name of his wife, yet we do know his own name was Alexander. I also know that his own son David who was this ship's Captain became a national hero.

During that war hundreds of brigs were made at North Shields and Howdon Docks. A strange place was Shields in that day - Haswell says in the 'Maister' - "A strange place too, the Shields of that day. Shut out from England, but in intimate touch with most of the stirring events occurring outside it. Hearing today of this or that Collier being taken by a Frenchman in the offing; seeing next day the ANTIGALLICAN beating up after plundering a score of sail. Scurrying down to the "Banks" to watch the frigate under tremendous press of sail mark down some unlucky foreign cruiser...... News travelled at best but slowly, and it was deemed neither necessary or desirable that "the people" should know anything of the affairs of the nation, the momentous events passed long before any tidings percolated down to the stratum. Just then, the whole English people was agog for news of Bonaparte, whose threatened invasion absorbed the public attention to the exclusion of most else."

Is it not strange that we do not hear the Wooden Dolly mentioned in the only book on North Shields - I mean the 'Maister' written in 1895 - is it that he too has thought it goes too far back that in his father's day no-one has recalled why it was placed there?

When the TOWN COMMISSIONERS swept away all the cannon - guns - figure heads - why was it they left this one alone? Was it not that they would have been lynched if they had attempted to take it away - and why?

In 1781, the rumour of invasion was frequent, for the combined fleets of France, Spain, Holland and the American Colonies, were much larger than our own Fleet. Many of our vessels were captured bound for Shields by a noted privateer Daniel Fall, the commander of the 'Fearnought'. The men on Tyne and Wear worked hard at the shipyards. Indeed, Britain was "all out" making munitions of War. On March 13th, that year, a frigate was launched at Monkwearmouth Shore called the 'Achilles', the sole property of James Stafford, mounting 28 pounders.

Could not the Shipbuilder, Mr. Bartleman do what Mr. Stafford had done? All we do know is that on June 7th, the Argo, of 44 guns was launched from Howdon Docks. It was the largest ship at that time launched on the River Tyne. Surely it is not far fetched to imagine Mr. Bartleman launching the 'Alexander and Margaret' of North Shields?

England in 1781. The enemies were masters of the Channel and the North Sea, both of which were literally swarming with Americans and French privateers. Commerce was at a standstill, the English Fleet helpless and the commanders could only hope to keep the enemy at bay.

Then a miracle did happen. Just after many vessels for Shields were captured by the noted privateer Daniel Fall, he turned and then attacked the 'Alexander and Margaret' and a terrible battle ensued. Fall was on the 'Fearnought', a ship of 18 four pounders. Mr. Bartleman's son, of North Shields, was ready to fight him against great odds. The battle really began near the Floating Light off Yarmouth; it lasted three hours. The enemy was beaten back three times, but, returning the fourth time, accomplished his object.

Young Captain Bartleman was severely wounded, while his mate was killed. The 'Alexander and Margaret' was hulled in about thirty places, and so was compelled to strike her colours. Being ransomed, she was taken into Yarmouth, where the injuries of brave Captain Bartleman received attention, but he died of wounds.

Bartleman, the hero, was given a public funeral. We can be assured his father went to that funeral - in any case he erected a tombstone in Yarmouth churchyard bearing the following inscription -

To the memory of David Bartleman, Master of the brig 'Alexander and Margaret' of North Shields. Who, on the 31st January, 1781, on the Norfolk Coast, with only 3, four pounders, and two men and two boys, nobly defended himself against a Cutter, carrying 18 four-pounders, and upwards of 100 men, commanded by the notorious English Pirate, Fall, and fairly beat him off. Two hours after the Enemy came down upon him again, when totally disabled. His Mate, Daniel Macauley, expiring with loss of blood, and himself dangerously wounded, he was obliged to strike and ransom. He brought his shattered ship into Yarmouth with more than the honour of a conqueror, and died here, in consequence of his wounds, on the 14th February following, in the 25th year of his age. To commemorate the gallantry of his son, the bravery of his faithful mate. And, at the same time, mark the infamy of a savage pirate, his afflicted father, Alexander Bartleman, has ordered this stone to be erected over his honourable grave, - "Twas great; His fee, though strong was infamous,

The fee of human kind. A man of indignation, his breast -Thank God, my son has done his duty."

Now if the father did not bring the figure head of his son's ship back to his native North Shields and place it in his garden - as a reminder of his son - then I'll eat nuts and forget the Wooden Dolly.

Rev. James Taggart

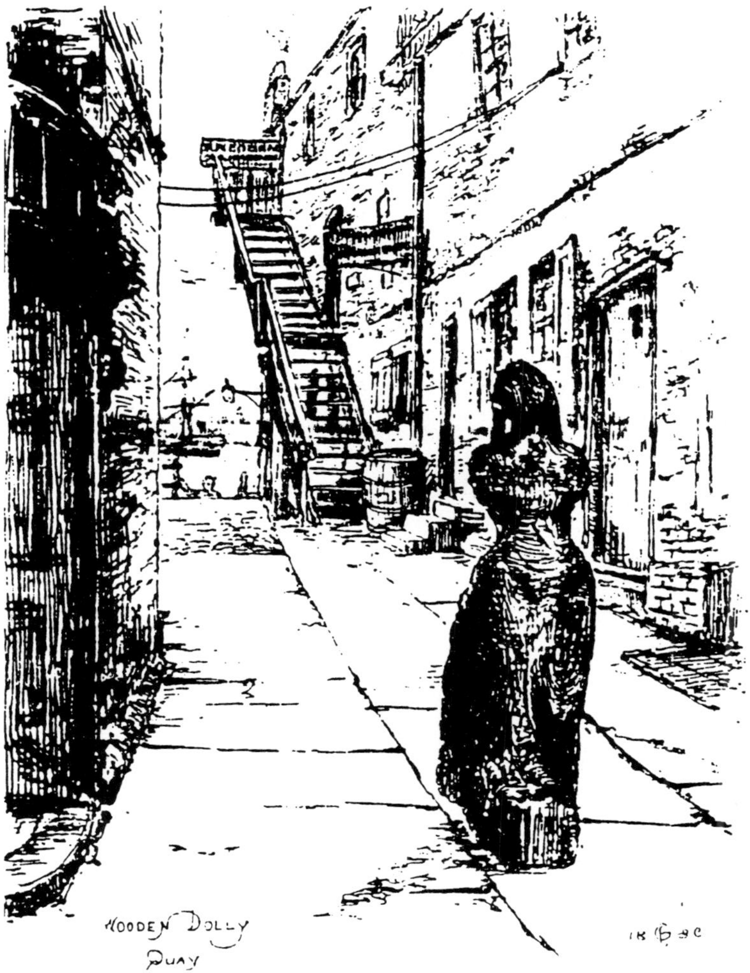

THE
MONTHLY
CHRONICLE
OF
NORTH-COUNTRY LORE AND LEGEND

323 *ENGRAVINGS.*

1890

Printed and Published for Proprietors of the "Newcastle Weekly Chronicle" by

WALTER SCOTT, NEWCASTLE-ON-TYNE,

AND 24 WARWICK LANE, PATERNOSTER ROW, LONDON.

The Wooden Dolly, North Shields.

DOLLY has stood in the Low Street, North Shields, through all the changes and vicissitudes incidental to the development and decay of an old seaport town over the past seventy or eighty years. And who is there, far and wide, that does not know her majestic form from personal observation? or, not knowing her, has not heard of her attractive charms by popular repute? So widespread and universal is her fair fame that old friendships have been renewed and cemented, mingled associations of pleasure and pain revived, and mutual introduction and intercourse effected, by the mere mention of the magic cognomen of the Wooden Dolly in almost every portion of the world into which the hardy Shields sailor has introduced his Tyneside dialect. Some there are who will be ready to dispute the fact that the Wooden Dolly has "braved the battle and the breeze" all through those long years. True, she has been patched, cleaned up, painted, renovated, re-fixed, and re-modelled. In fact, so near had her venerable form approached utter demolition at one time by a species of "Dolly worship" that seized hold upon our superstitious sons of Neptune and induced

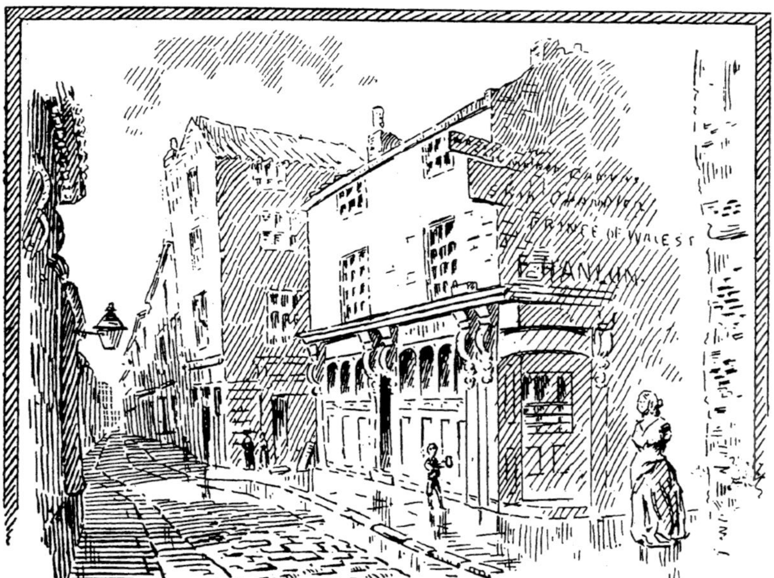

The Wooden Dolly, the Low Street, North Shields.

them to chip off pieces of the figure to carry over the main with them as a sort of charm against the perils to which their calling exposed them, that many believe that she was, some score years or so back, rejuvenated and reimbued with all her stately disposition of drapery and other feminine adornments from a "breaking-up yard."

It is sufficient to state that there has been a Wooden Dolly standing in the position of the present one, uninterruptedly, over very many years, with the exception, so far as can be learned, of an hour or so upon an occasion when some carousing shipwrights and naval reserve men carried her away, "lock, stock, and barrel," and placed her at the foot of the Wooden Bridge Bank, at a time when there was but a very narrow roadway there, doubtless as a protest against the passage of vehicular traffic along the narrow and circuitous thoroughfares branching off on either hand. Dolly's origin, and the purpose which she was intended to serve when she was placed there, have always been debatable points. The most natural theory is that long ago, when the Custom House Quay—more popularly known as the Wooden Dolly Quay—was formed, the Dolly was placed at its entrance to preserve the right of way, and to prevent the introduction of vehicular traffic.* Everything round about seems to have incorporated itself with the personality of the Dolly. Custom House Quay has become Wooden Dolly Quay ; Custom House Steps have become Wooden Dolly Steps ; and the Prince of Wales Hotel, within reach of Dolly's right arm, if she were able to utilise it for the purpose of slaking her thirst, has lost its royal identity in the course of the popular homage, and is now much better known as the Wooden Dolly "public-hoose."

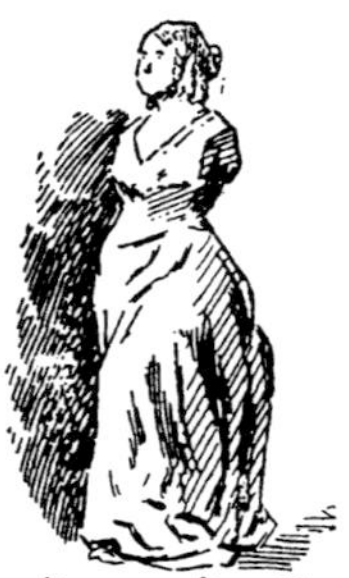

Wooden Dolly

Dolly has always been a sort of landmark by which to direct the inquiring stranger to his destination. She was at one time, too, turned to practical account by being ruthlessly subjected to the indignity of having a warp turned round her ankles for the purpose of drawing heavy spars and baulks of timber up the quay. Her career has been in a great measure made noteworthy by the affection and endearments that have been lavished upon her by the seafaring population. Sailors coming home after long voyages, after having got "half-seas over," have frequently been known to hug and kiss her as fervently as they would an ancient female relative. Others who have succeeded in getting into a really "heavy sea," and, staggering along under all canvas, have rolled up against her, have been known to "sheer off" with an oath ; but immediately afterwards, on discovering their mistake, have pulled up with a lurch and a "Hollo, old gal, ish't you aa's broached ? Well, hoo ye gettin' on, eh ? Come an' hev a drink, old gal !" Dolly proving obdurate to the allurements of gallant Jack, occasions have been known where he, with characteristic determination to "do the amiable," has entered the house at the corner, and, returning with a glass of steaming spirits, has poured its contents over her upturned face. Others in a like predicament, who have not been favoured with her personal acquaintance, have frequently ordered her to "shiver her timbers." And so the fun has gone on over a longer time than the proverbial "oldest inhabitant" can remember.

Although young children have always regarded Dolly with a certain amount of awe, and their parents have held her in respect and veneration, the "hobbledehoy" has frequently had to be taken to task for exercising his natural propensity for slashing and carving at everything with his pocket-knife; and so often was her aquiline nose shaved off flat with her face that it was found necessary to impose a fine on a youth who had despoiled her. After this salutary lesson, Dolly underwent a somewhat rough and unsurgical operation that resulted in her appearing the following morning with a metal nose, which was screwed into its place, and has to this day defeated the efforts of her implacable enemy, the boy with a knife.

Public attention was attracted towards Dolly to an unusual degree awhile ago. It arose from the fact that mine host of the adjoining hostelry had taken practical steps to have her placed in a state of becoming repair, and to that end had engaged workmen to fill in the decayed and mutilated portions of her figure with cement, during which unnatural process she was made to accept the prevailing fashion as to the arrangement of her drapery by the addition of an "improver." Her new dress of emerald green gave unqualified satisfaction to the greater portion of the residents in the neighbourhood, who evinced the liveliest interest in the proceedings. Dolly, if left alone, is now in condition to last for many a year to come.

* A correspondent of the *Weekly Chronicle* (William Street, North Shields) confirms this theory, adding one or two other items of interest. "I am," he says, "unable to give the exact date, but, about the year 1814, Mr. Alexander Bartleman owned an old collier brig that was being put into dock for repairs, and while here the figure-head was taken off and placed where the present Dolly stands. The purpose for which it was placed there was to prevent vehicles backing down the quay and causing inconvenience to business people at that place. There were previously posts, or a bar, across the quay. At the time the figure was first placed in position there was a small garden plot on the Custom House Quay, and also trees growing upon it—not trees that grow in a flower pot, but trees nearly as high as the house tops."

THE WOODEN DOLLY.
OFFER OF A NEW ONE

Last night a meeting was held at the Seven Stars Inn, Bell Street, North Shields, to consider what steps might be taken with a view to erecting a new Wooden Dolly on the site of the old one. Mr. J. Frater presided. Mr. G. H. Blagburn, of North Shields, stated that he would provide a ship's figurehead in place of the old Dolly. The matter was fully discussed, and it was eventually thought that the figurehead offered by Mr. Blagburn would be too large for the limited space at the place where the Dolly stood. However, the Chairman consented to examine the figure head in question to see definitely whether or not it would be suitable, and Mr. Blagburn was thanked for his offer. A sub-committee, consisting of the chairman, Mr. Fairweather, Mr. Harvey, Mr. Dunn and Mr. Dunleavy, was appointed for the purpose of making inquiries as to the procuring of a figure head of a suitable size, and also to consider the advisability of purchasing a metal Dolly, and dispensing with the wooden one altogether.

Shields Daily News 17th July, 1900

UNVEILING THE WOODEN DOLLY

The new wooden Dolly, which was carved some time since by Miss Spence, daughter of the late Ald. J. F. Spence, and which was a few days ago placed upon the site of the old one, was unveiled yesterday morning amid much enthusiasm. A procession was formed at the Town Hall, where the bands of the Wellesley Training Ship, and the Tynemouth Union, under Bandmaster Shutt and W. Sharp, had assembled. Large crowds of persons followed the bands to the site of the Dolly, which is situate at the corner of Custom House Quay, Liddell Street, and in the twinkling of an eye the narrow thoroughfare was completely blocked from end to end, and the liveliest interest was taken in the proceedings. Mr. W. Chapman presided, and amongst others present were Mr. John Frater, Chairman of the committee; County Ald. J. H. Hogg, Councillors J. Eskdale and G.M. Hogg, Mr. W.H. Park, and Mr. Sep. Scott, clerk to the Guardians. There were several members of the Boys' Brigade also present.

The CHAIRMAN made an appropriate speech in opening the proceedings, his sentiments regarding the popularity of the Wooden Dolly being punctuated with applause.

County Alderman J. R. HOGG, on being called upon to perform the unveiling ceremony, made an impressive reference to the illness of the King, and said that the great heart of the nation to its uttermost extremity beat in sympathy with the devoted wife and family in their great trouble, and they were all united in a common hope and prayer that the Being in whose hands was the destiny of kings as well as of peasants, would yet restore the King to his wonted health. He joined them in the regret that Mr. James Knott was unable to be present, and expressed his belief that Shields people had many reasons to be proud of Mr. Knott. But though he said it who shouldn't, there were two qualifications which he possessed, and which he thought ought to be possessed by anyone performing that ceremony. In the first place he though he ought to be a Shieldsman - (Applause) - and he himself was born within five minutes from where they stood. (Cheers.) He took no credit for that fact. (Laughter.) He was never consulted about it, but it was a fact of which he was proud. (Applause.) Then he possessed a second qualification, and in that he yielded to no man, it is an intense regard for the town of his birth and for its ancient landmarks. He believed in a patriotism which while being national was also local, and included their own town and their own calf yard. (Applause.) He had travelled in many lands and seen many of the finest spots in the world, but he said it from the bottom of his heart that he saw no place he liked so well as North Shields. (Loud cheers.) Now the Wooden Dolly was just one of those instances which fastened themselves round the memory and the imagination. He had met old Shields men in many parts of the world, and there was one question they generally asked, that was, "Is the Wooden Dolly still there?" (Cheers.) The history of the Dolly was that in 1814 Mr. Alex. Bartleman had a collier brig in to repair. Previous to that time there was a bar at the top of the quay to prevent carts backing down. Mr. Bartleman removed the bar and placed there the figurehead of the ship. How many Dollies there had been he did not know. A gentleman yesterday told him he had seen four, but the last one was erected on June 20, 1864, upon the day the foundation stone of the old Low Lights Dock was laid. It was the figurehead of the 'Expert,' a boat which belonged to Messrs. J. I. Wait. Having unveiled the dolly amidst loud and prolonged cheers, Mr. Hogg paid a high tribute to the work and to the carver of the image, Miss Spence, daughter of the late Ald. John Foster Spence. Former Wooden Dollies, if they could speak, could tell of great changes. They witnessed that Low Street as the most important commercial street in the town. They saw it crowded with jolly jack tars, who were sailors in reality as well as in name. They saw the decline of the sailing ship, and the rise and development of the steam ship. He hoped the present Wooden Dolly would continue to be a landmark in an ever increasingly successful town, and to many generations of prosperous, sober, contented, and happy Shields people. (Loud and continued applause.)

Ald. HOGG then ordered the figure to be disclosed whereupon the wooden box with which she was covered was removed amid the lusty cheers of the multitude and the spirited playing of the bands.

Mr. J. FRATER, in a few well chosen sentences, moved a vote of thanks to Ald. Hogg.

Mr. W. H. PARK seconded the motion, which was supported by Coun. ESKDALE, and carried with hearty acclamation.

At the close of the ceremony the crowd swarmed up the bank, which extends from the Library Flags to Liddell Street, in order that they might have a view of the sports which had been arranged by Mr. W. H. Park. It is a large open space covered with the debris of ruined and demolished property, and in a very short space of time it was covered with one solid mass of humanity. Every available coign of vantage in the vicinity was also freely taken advantage of, and not a little risk was run by the more venturesome, who scaled giddy heights and rickety buildings in their eagerness to witness the proceedings. A capital programme had been arranged, the events including a greasy pole competition, boxing contests for the boys, ducking for oranges, bun and treacle competition, &c., and a wonderful amount of fun was introduced by the competitors. In the boxing contests there was much to excite the risible faculties. A proper platform had been erected, and a large bath filled with water occupied a position in the corner. This was to be used in the "ducking" competition, but it served another purpose. Two youngsters were engaged in a lively bout, one being a member of the Boys' Brigade. The contest became slightly heated, and it was just nearing its conclusion when suddenly the Boys' Brigade member shot out and into the bath went his opponent. He was pulled out and presented a woeful appearance. The incident could be seen by everyone of the six thousand people congregated on the banks, and the loud laughter which it evoked might have been heard for miles. The proceedings were rendered additionally enjoyable by the playing of the bands of the Wellesley and the Tynemouth Union, the conductors of which deserve every credit for the able performances of their pupils. At the close the prizes were presented to the successful competitors by Mr. W. Lindsey. The arrangements were admirably carried out under the direction of Mr. W. H. Park, who worked most enthusiastically to bring the affair to a successful issue.

Shields Daily News 27th June, 1902

THE OLD WOODEN DOLLY AT THE CUSTOM HOUSE QUAY

The Old Wooden Dolly - not the present one - she was no slim, simpering goddess-looking creature, as if she had just stepped from the frieze of the Parthenon, but a bluff, sousie, hearty-looking hussey, with a full flaunty petticoat, something in style of good Queen Bess. She had been a nice looking hussey in her time, - she could bear a look, and never change colour - never blushed, though exposed to the gaze of the public from morning till night. It was beside her that that wonderful man used to stand, on the night of the 30th of December, who had as many noses as there were days in the year; he generally stood just in front, with his hands in his jacket pockets. You could see him for the trouble of going so far. I have seen him myself a hundred times, nay that number of a hundred must be taken figuratively. I am not yet quite a hundred years old.

That Memnon of ancient Egypt was a stupid affair, not at all to be compared to the wooden woman at the Custom House Quay. It merely emitted a musical sound when struck by the first ray of the sun. But the wooden woman once spoke - no mistake, none whatever - it was at the witching hour of night, the town clock had told twelve, when Jonathan Squeezebottle, he clasped the wooden woman in his arms, either from sheer affection or to prevent himself from measuring his length on the pavement, when Lo! Mirabile dictu, that wooden woman spoke:-

"What d'ye say?" said Jonathan. "What are you talking about?"

"Go home, Jonathan," said the wooden woman.

"What were you talking about?" hiccoughed Jonathan.

"Jonathan Squeezebottle, go home," said she.

"Well, well," said Jonathan, "good advice should always be followed." So he turned upon his heel to make the best of his way home.

"Good-night," said he.

"Good-night, Jonathan Squeezebottle," said the wooden woman.

Now it has been suggested that it was someone standing behind the wooden woman who spoke to Jonathan: but such a supposition is highly preposterous - Jonathan knew better than that.

It was near the wooden woman that the inhabitants of Shields were initiated into the mysteries of gas lighting. When they were laying the pipes in the streets, one of the oldest inhabitants came to see.

"Eh! what new things are always coming up, Tony," said she, addressing a little round-faced old man, who was standing with his back against the wooden woman, "will they bring the gas light through the pipes from the Low Lights, just the same way as they bring the water?"

"Yes," said Tony, with his usual briskness of manner, "there's to be a pant beside the wooden woman, where they'll run it out at the top, and sell it at so much a gallon."

"Eh! hinny, Tony," says she, "that will be clever, we'll come and get a little sup of gaslight in a pot whenever we want a light, and then we can always keep a little sup in the closet to be ready."

Strong arguments were held beside the wooden woman, long conversations were held beside the wooden woman, long stories were told beside the wooden woman.

A batch of old sailors would often take their stand beside her on an afternoon. You might often hear something similar to the following dialogue among them:

"In the year fourteen, when it was such a hard frost."

"That's a lie, there was no frost at all in the year fourteen!"

"What do you know about it? You weren't born the year fourteen!"

"Want a boat, sir? Go off with you directly."

"It's not your turn. Don't you know it's mine."

"I know better than that!"

"But I know better!"

"Who do you follow?"

"I follow Tom."

"No! I follow Tom."

"I know better!"

"--- You know nothing about it!"

It is related of one of these worthies that he took a voyage to London in his scullerboat, rowing merrily along when the weather was fine, and creeping into shelter when the weather was foul. He had served a considerable time on board men-of-war, and received a very good pension. His only object in going so far was to see some old acquaintances in Wapping.

After a few days of fun and wild enjoyment, he returned the same way, calling at all the ports along the coast, and spending a day here and a night there.

One night about the witching hour of twelve a party who had just risen from their cups (this is the end of the chapter) observed and old acquaintance, half seas over, seated on a stone step opposite the wooden woman, and addressing her thus:

"Go home, go home, you're like nobody else, never in the house, out on the street night after night. Go home, I say, go home!"

You may judge how like a woman she was, when this poor fellow had mistaken her for his wife.

"Go home," says he, "go home, - will you not go home? Will you not go home when I tell yon? Go home, - go home!"

"Go home," said one of the wags, giving her a drive, "go home and go to bed with your husband. Go home."

"Go home, you idle slut," said another, giving her a punch on the other side.

"Make her go home," said another, "carry her home, whether she will or not," and setting themselves to work, they actually tore the poor woman out of the ground.

"Try if she be willing to walk now," said one, "and if not, carry her shoulder high."

But the poor feeble old body, either from age or incapacity, or sheer obstinacy, fell flat on her nose.

"Up with her," said one or two, "up with her and carry her home to bed."

Mounting her upon their shoulders, they carried her as far as the Wooden Bridge, when one or two of them making a stagger in the street, she was precipitated to the ground, and by that fall her neck was broken. She was found in the same place next morning, and her head was made use of to prop up her body and prevent it rolling into the street. What became of her after that I really do not know. Whether they dug a grave for her and buried her decently, or whether, like Patrocles, the friend of Achilles, she was consumed to ashes. The latter is the most likely.

Shields Daily News 24th June, 1910

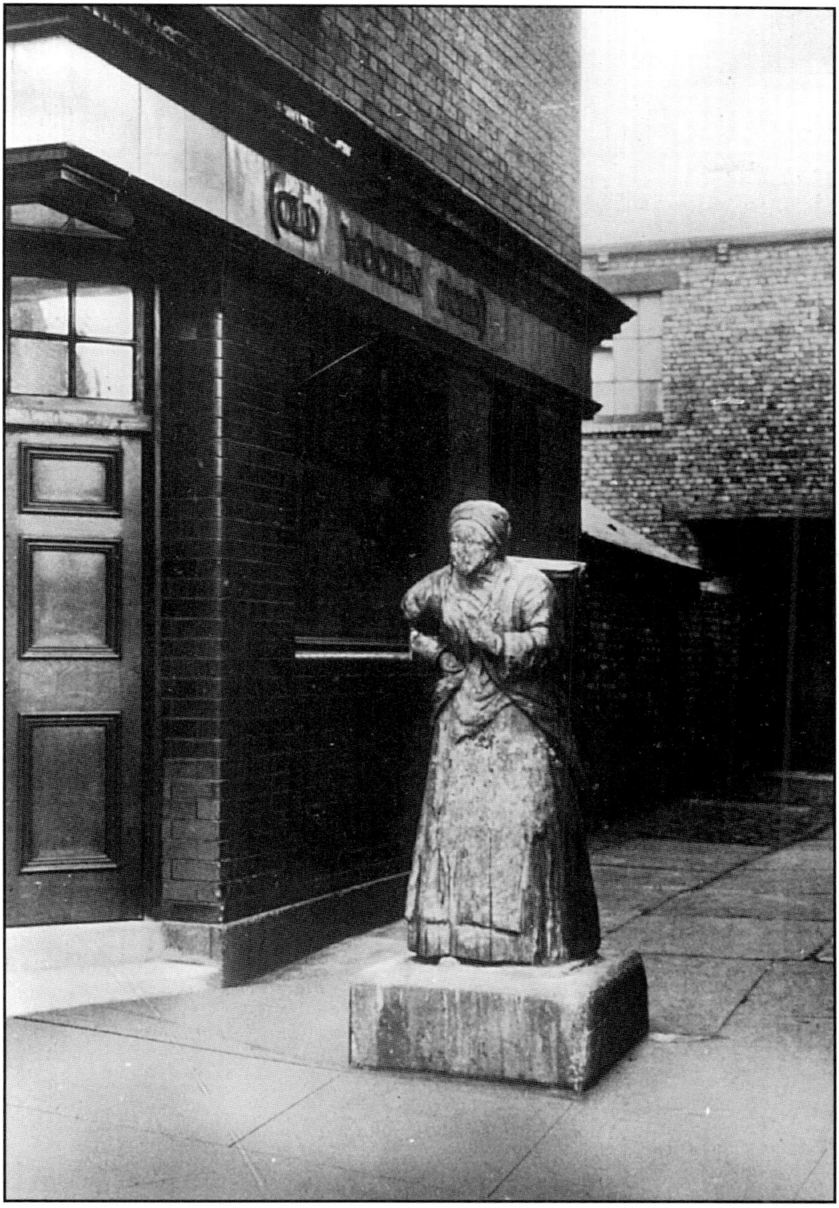

Wooden Dolly 4

The fifth Wooden Dolly currently standing in Northumberland Square, North Shields, was carved in the workshop of Robert Thompson, famous for his mouse trademark. Here is a brief outline of his life and work.

THE MOUSE MAN

On May 7, 1876, at the Old Hall in the North Yorkshire village of Kilburn, the wife of the local joiner and wheelwright gave birth to a son whose work in ecclesiological surroundings, stately homes, civic buildings, public schools, colleges and humble country inns was to be synonymous with unblemished craftsmanship and pride of achievement. The work displayed the famous mouse trademark of the master carver - Robert Thompson.

How did the mouse come into being? In a letter dated February 10, 1949, Robert told his own story. His correspondent was the Rector of Berkeley, Gloucestershire.

Dear Sir,

Priest's Stall, Berkeley

I beg to thank you, most sincerely for your lovely and kind words of appreciation. I value this far more than the money.

Also I am so pleased to hear that my work occupies such a beautiful setting. Somehow, I don't enjoy doing work for modern churches.

The origin of the mouse as my mark was almost in the way of being an accident. I and another carver were carving a huge cornice for a Screen and happened to say something about being as poor as a church mouse. I said: I'll carve a mouse here and did so. Then it struck me, what a lovely trade mark. This is about 30 years ago.

Our vicar asked me what was its meaning. I said: "It means industry in a quiet place." He said: "Nay, man, destruction."

Again thanking you for your kind words.

Yours very truly,

R. Thompson.

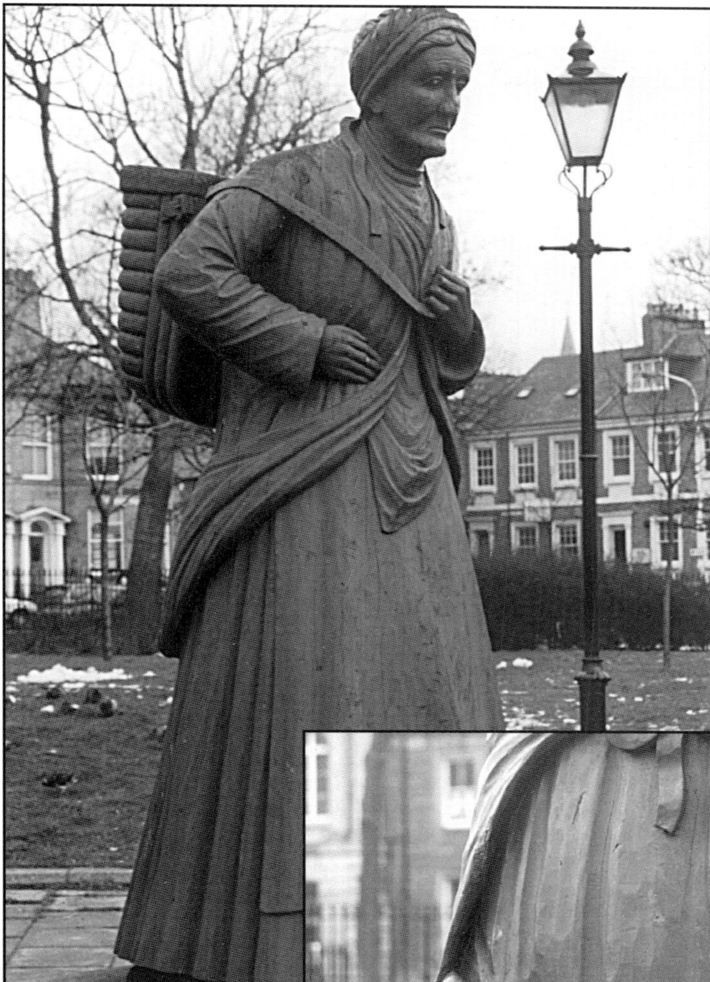

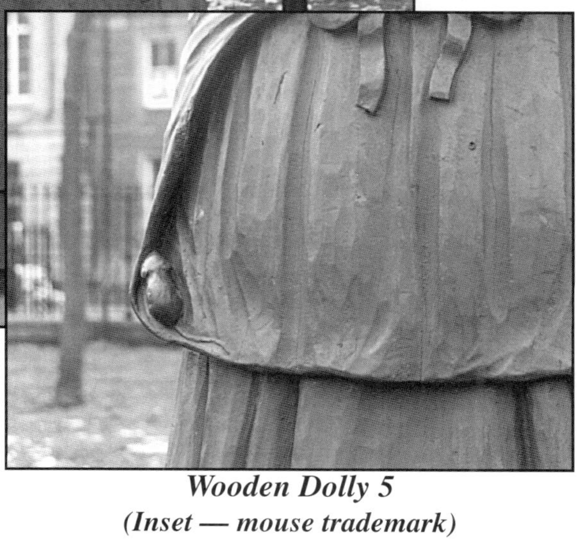

Wooden Dolly 5
(Inset — mouse trademark)

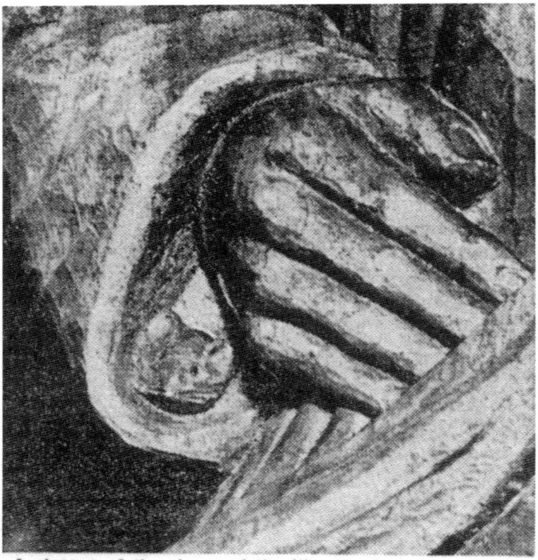

A closeup of the sleeve of the Wooden Dolly showing the mouse insignia used by Robt. Thompson's Craftsmen Ltd., of Kilburn, who carved the effigy—there is another mouse also featured on the carving.

His grandsons have enlarged on this theme by naming the carver who made the embryonic utterance as Charlie Barker and placing the date of the first mouse as the early 1920s. They cannot say which church Thompson was repairing, and it is a strange thing that the first mouse has never been definitely located. A trademark that has become a legend is elusive as to its birthplace.

His woodcarving of the highest order is found in 700 cathedrals and churches, including Westminster Abbey, York Minster and Benedictine Abbeys, together with stately homes and council chambers, schools and colleges, not forgetting the innumerable north country inns who are proud to point out in their dining rooms the significance of the many "mice" which are dotted about the tables and chairs.

Robert Thompson was still carving at 79 years of age. He was a perfectionist to the end. He was laid to rest on December 11, 1955, behind the squat brown tower of the church beside his Kilburn workshop. He had lived a life of nearly 80 years of creative work, a life for which he himself had chosen the motto "Industry in Quiet Places."

Jas. Thompson

(Extract from'The Dalesman', April 1976)

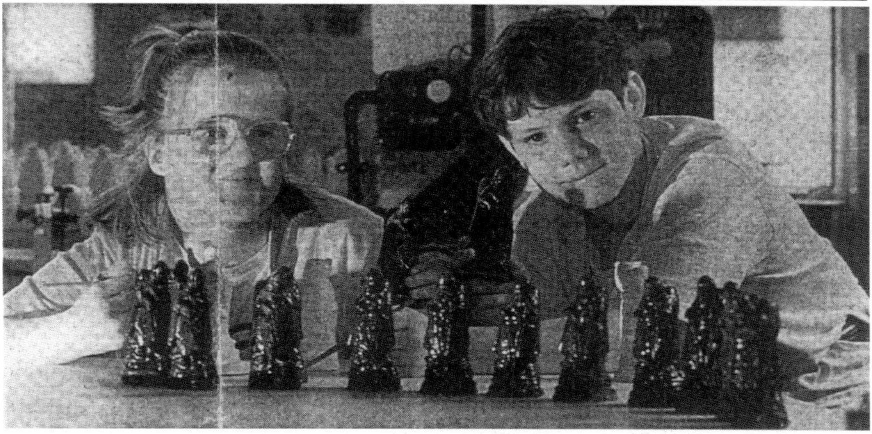

Glebe School pupils Louise Smith and Paul Rayner with some of the models ready to sell at the Fish Quay Festival

Dolly is a chip off old block

ONE of Tyneside' most famous figures is set to make a hit at her home town's Fish Quay Festival — and help local school children.

More than 500 models of North Shields' Wooden Dolly made by pupils at Glebe School, Killingworth, will be on sale at the quayside event this weekend.

It is the biggest order yet for the school which caters for children with moderate learning needs between the ages of four and 16.

Two years ago the technology department launched a business called Bits and Bobs after school governor and North Shields trader Joe Morrison bought two original moulds of the Wooded Dolly.

He ordered 40 plaster figures to be sold at the North Shields Fish Quay Festival, with 100 going the following year. The venture is now so successful that 500 will be up for grabs at this bank holiday weekend at the fifth festival. More than a dozen youngsters are involved with Bits and Bobs although many of the school's 100 pupils help.

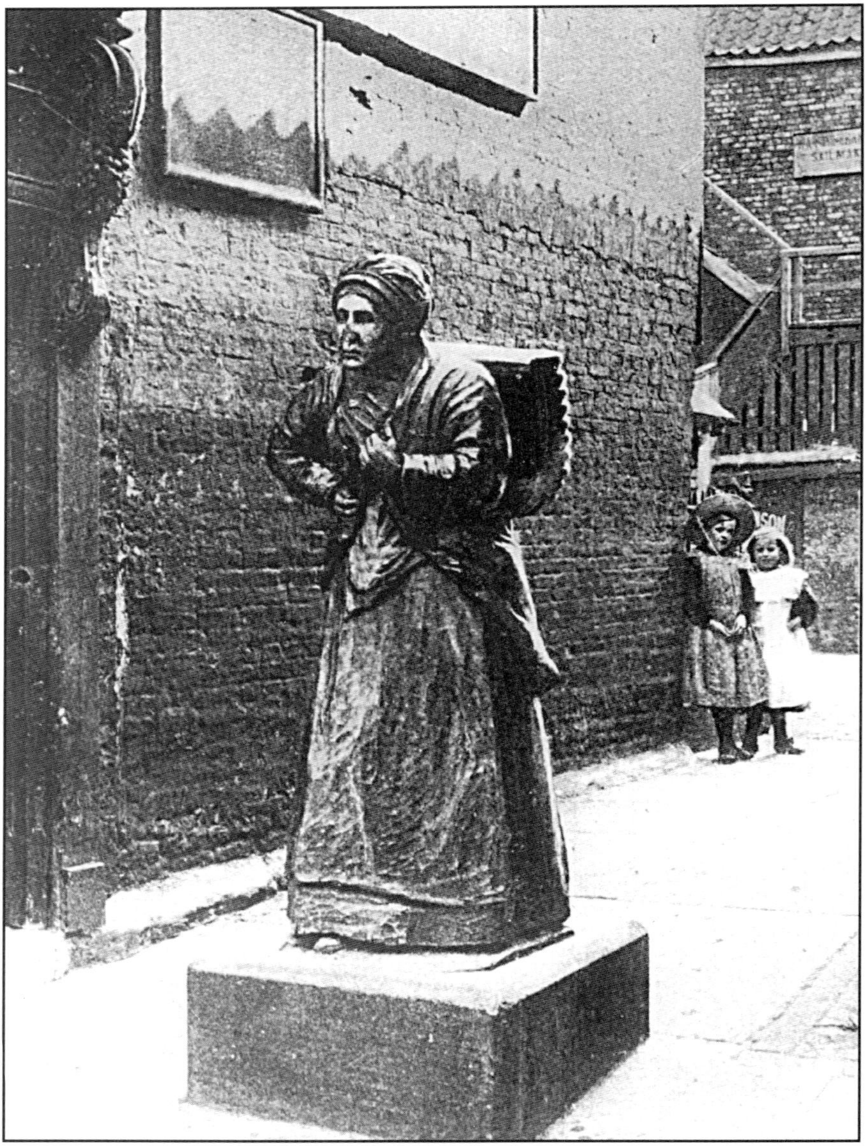

Wooden Dolly 4

The Shields Daily News

DOLLY LETTERS

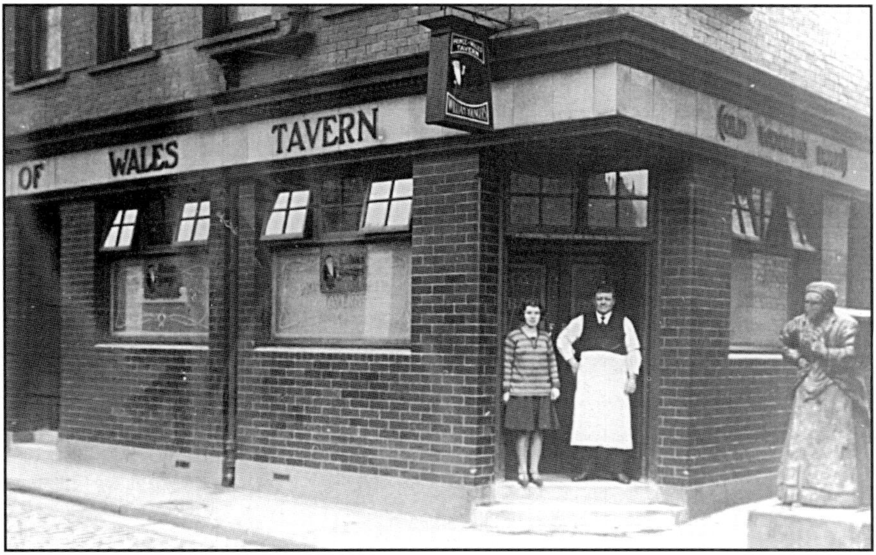

Wooden Dolly 4

Letters to the Editor

THE WOODEN DOLLY

SIR, - It is now two years since I last informed you of my open wounds and wretched condition, and I am sorry to say I am as yet unrepaired, but the time has at last arrived when I must be either renovated or replaced. In explaining the services of self and ancestors, I may say that no freeman of Newcastle-on Tyne ever kept better watch and ward than we have done, for I can swear and declare that no horse and carts have ever crossed the precincts over which we have had jurisdiction for so many years.

An architect has estimated that this once lovely form may be again made beautiful for, say £5.10s, a small sum considering the utility of myself. I may suggest that my skirts be widened to prevent boys wheeling barrows down the quay, it not only injures the respectability of the neighbourhood but soils my dress. I should have liked a brass face, but I live in the vicinity of several old metallurgists, and some fine morning I might awake to find myself *defaced*.

I thought of asking the Town Council for a coat of paint, but having heard they have allowed a coal spout on the New Quay to blacken the burgesses, I cannot now ask them to stultify themselves. I appeal specially to those who make a landmark of me, those who, after a night's carouse, have steadied themselves against me and whispered most endearing words of love into my ears, in mistake for a more animated being. In thus appealing for subscriptions I hope I shall hurt the feelings of none, but enlist the sympathy of the many. This is no Ortonian humbug, but a case of real distress and visible mutilation. A considerable sum has been already subscribed. The lists lay at the shop o' my kind neighbour, Mr. Murphy, who will gladly receive all donations. Apologising for troubling you,

I remain, yours truly,

THE WOODEN DOLLY

North Shields, 27th April, 1874

TO THE MEMORY OF THE "WOODEN DOLLY"

Whence, her name and history, it suits me not to say,
Suffice it, that perchance they were of fame,
And had been glorious in another day:- Byron.

SIR - One of the few historic street marks of North Shields has disappeared, or, to be more correct, is rapidly doing so - in short the "Wooden Dolly" has disappeared from the waist upwards. On looking at what remains, the words of Byron come to mind.

Shades of the might! can it be,
That this is all remains of thee.

The poor old lady has summered and wintered the none too generous weather of North Shields for a long time. She has also withstood the embraces and assaults of all sorts and conditions of humanity, until "fatal day," some "cuss broke her in halfs." Alas! poor Dolly - her virtues were many, and her faults few. At national or local subscriptions she was there with her box. She afforded to the tippler an outlet for his amorous or pugnacious qualities, also a certain amount of amusement. The small boy of the neighbourhood loved her for various reasons. On dark and foggy nights she was there to welcome the sailor man to his steps. The Medusa boys will miss her, at least the cook says so. Mr. Editor, cannot we do something to replace her? Let us re-erect her. I am a spiritualist.

Yours etc.,
COOK'S MATE

North Shields, 21st June, 1900

I am sure that a very general feeling of regret would be felt throughout the Borough at the announcement that our old friend the Wooden Dolly had come to grief. On learning the sad news myself I undertook a pilgrimage to the Low Street, and found the report only too true. There is now no Wooden Dolly - only a rather ghastly-looking stump to remind the passers by of her untimely end. The rotten condition of the wood bears witness to the strain which weather and old age had put upon the familiar figurehead, and one wished that more gentle treatments had been accorded the quaint relic than seems to have been its fate. How the demolition came to pass history doth not record. Let us hope it was by some accident. The individual who could wantonly destroy this familiar landmark deserves badly of the town, and had I my Ruskin by me I could hurl at him some vigorous denunciations of the wickedness of destroying historical erections, which belong to the past, present, and future generations alike, and to tamper with which is to "take what isn't his'n." However, it was perhaps scarcely to be expected that the Wooden Dolly would last indefinitely, though her demise is much to be regretted as breaking one of the links which join modern Shields to the picturesque, far-away days of the old town. The Wooden Dolly stood at a particularly prosaic-looking part of the Low Street, and to come suddenly upon the queer, grim old image was to be reminded in strong contrast of the period when wood had not yet given place to iron. There is plenty of interesting literature, happily, to be resorted to for accounts of Shields life early in the century, and a stirring picture it is. Of varieties of language and costume in the street itself, and of build and rig of ships in the river beyond, there was no end, and the babel that went on within its narrow bounds was scarcely to be matched the world over. In fact, the people were believed then to know a great deal more about outlandish parts than they knew about their own country. From those days the fall of the Wooden Dolly helps to separate us still further, though apart from picturesque effect there is no reason to regret the change. And even if we get a new "Dolly" will not the spell remain broken?

North Shields, 25th June, 1900

THE WOODEN WOMAN AT THE CUSTOM HOUSE QUAY

SIR, - I was not a little surprised the other day to notice in your paper that the Wooden Woman at the Custom House Quay had come to so untimely an end, as I believed her constitution to have been good for many years to come.

The Town Clerk of Tynemouth, Mr. H. A. Adamson, has kindly mentioned in the *Daily News* that perhaps I may be able to give some facts concerning the Wooden Dolly, but I am afraid I can add but little to what has already appeared in the local papers.

The Custom House Quay is said to have been formed in the year 1774, and it is supposed the Wooden Dolly was placed at its entrance at that time. This is not correct.

In my letter to the *Weekly Chronicle*, Feb. 22nd, 1890, I stated that I was unable to give the exact date, but about the year 1814 Mr. Alexander Bartleman owned an old collier brig that was being put into dock for repairs, and, while here, the figure head was taken off and placed where the recent figure stood. The purpose for which it was placed there was to prevent vehicles from backing down the quay, causing inconvenience to business people at that place. There had previously been posts, or a bar, across the Quay, but these obstacles had been frequently knocked down, hence the placing of the Wooden Dolly there. At the time the figure was first placed in position, there was a small garden plot on the quay, and also trees growing upon it, not trees that grow in a flower pot, but trees nearly as high as the house tops.

Paul Trumpeter, in "Things that Were," in his story of the wooden woman, says she was no slim, simpering, Goddess-looking creature, but a bluff, saucy, hearty-looking hussey, with a full flaunting petticoat something in the style of a good Queen Bess. She could bear a look and never change colour. He tells us that a party just risen from their cups addressed Dolly, and advised her to go home, which advice she respectfully declined. They actually tore the poor old woman out of the ground and carried her shoulder high to the Wooden Bridge, when, one or two of them making a stagger in the street, she was precipitated to the ground, and by that fall her neck was broken. She was found in the same place next morning, and the head was made use of to prop up the body. What became of her after that is not known. Probably she was cremated. Thus ends Dolly No. 1.

The second Dolly was placed in the position of the first one, by one Mr. Hare, a sailmaker, whose business was down that quay, but I am unable to say at what date it was placed there.

Dolly No. 3, who has so suddenly come to disaster was formerly the figure head of the barque Expert, belonging to John and James Wait, of

Northumberland Square, and in 1864 was sold to Mr. Stevenson, Duke Street, North Shields, who, while the vessel was in dock for repairs, had the outwater and figure head removed.

Mr. H. Strong and Mr. Harkus, block and mast makers, Dock Landing, Liddell Street, made some new spars for the Expert while she was being repaired, and Mr. Stevenson gave them the figure-head. The Expert was some years, previous to being sold to Mr. Stevenson, commanded by Mr. Thomas Driver, late pawnbroker, of Linskill Street, from whom I got this information.

The 23rd of June 1864 (just 36 years ago) was the day on which the foundation stone of the Low Lights Dock was laid, and, as it was supposed a new era was about to dawn upon the town of North Shields, it was considered an appropriate time for the placing of this beautiful figure, which was considered a fine work of art, in lieu of the old one then standing. The figure was placed securely in the ground by Mr. John Harkus and James Pringle on the previous evening (that is, June 22nd), without any ceremony whatever, but on the following morning an agreeable surprise was in store for the many passers-by who stopped to admire this handsome Wooden Lady. The figure had not been set up many years before the Low Street arabs and other mischievous persons had hacked poor Dolly's nose in such a manner as to leave her almost noseless. At last, skilled art was called in to supply the defect, and Mr. Robert Pow, at that time a well-known blacksmith in Liddell Street, was the person to whom the remodelling of Dolly's nose was entrusted. This he accomplished by inserting an iron one, which up to the time of her demise had stood the test of all the hacking and rough usage to which Dolly has been subjected.

I never hear mention of the Wooden Dolly Quay but it reminds me of the stories I have heard or read concerning this place of press gang notoriety. Joe Fiddler formerly kept the public house at the top of the Quay, and immediately opposite on the other side of the street, and on which Dolly always had her eye, stood another public house, The Admiral Nelson. In 1827 this house was kept by William Bothwick, whose wife survived him and carried on the business for some time afterwards, successfully. The Admiral Nelson was a noted house for stout, and it was said that -

The best champagne
Or wines from Spain,
Or choicest liquors out,
Could not indeed
In taste exceed
Sweet Nancy Bothwick's stout.

Nancy Bothwick became quite a household name. No stout was like Nancy's London stout, and a rare business she did in that commodity, both on and off the premises. Masters of ships frequented Nancy's parlour to transact their business, and quaff their stout from bright pewter pots. Nancy was a sprightly widow, of jolly disposition, neat and clean, and always dressed in black, and was rather corpulent. The regular frequenters of Nancy's establishment each had his own pipe stowed away in its own private place, ready to be brought out to him as he entered. Here the old-fashioned tin pipestand stood upon the table well loaded for those who liked to enjoy their yard of clay.

Almost every nook and corner from the Low Lights to the Lime Kiln Shore has its little history.

Ah! happy years! Once more, who would not be a boy?

I am afraid I have trespassed far beyond the limit allotted to a correspondent, but hoping you may be pleased to find space in your columns for this letter.`

I remain, sir, yours respectfully,

WILLIAM STREET

North Shields, 30th June, 1900

THE WOODEN DOLLY

SIR, - I was astonished on seeing, to-day, in Mr. Park's window, the wood carving by Miss Spence, intended for renewal of our Wooden Dolly. I, during a long life, have given some attention to works of art, and I went just for curiosity, but found one of the most extraordinary figures I have ever clapped eyes on. To think for one moment of placing such on the place of the old Dolly seems to me preposterous, the more especially coming from the lady bearing the name of Spence.

Our townsmen will make a mistake if they allow it be placed there. It is a credit to the town, and, although it was intended originally for that position, I feel sure this difficulty could easily be got over. And to show my earnestness in this matter, if our worthy Mayor would take it up and a suitable site were found, I have no objection to head the list with a substantial subscription.

Yours,

D. A. N.

North Shields, 18th Dec. 1901

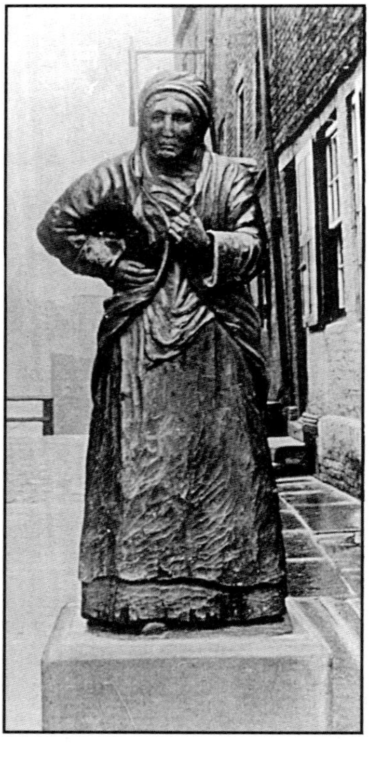

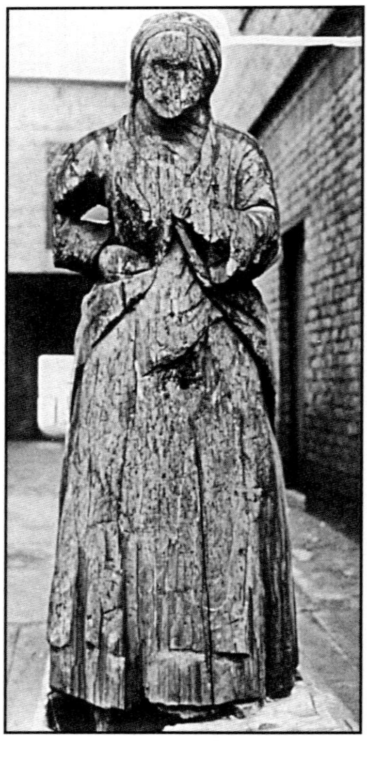

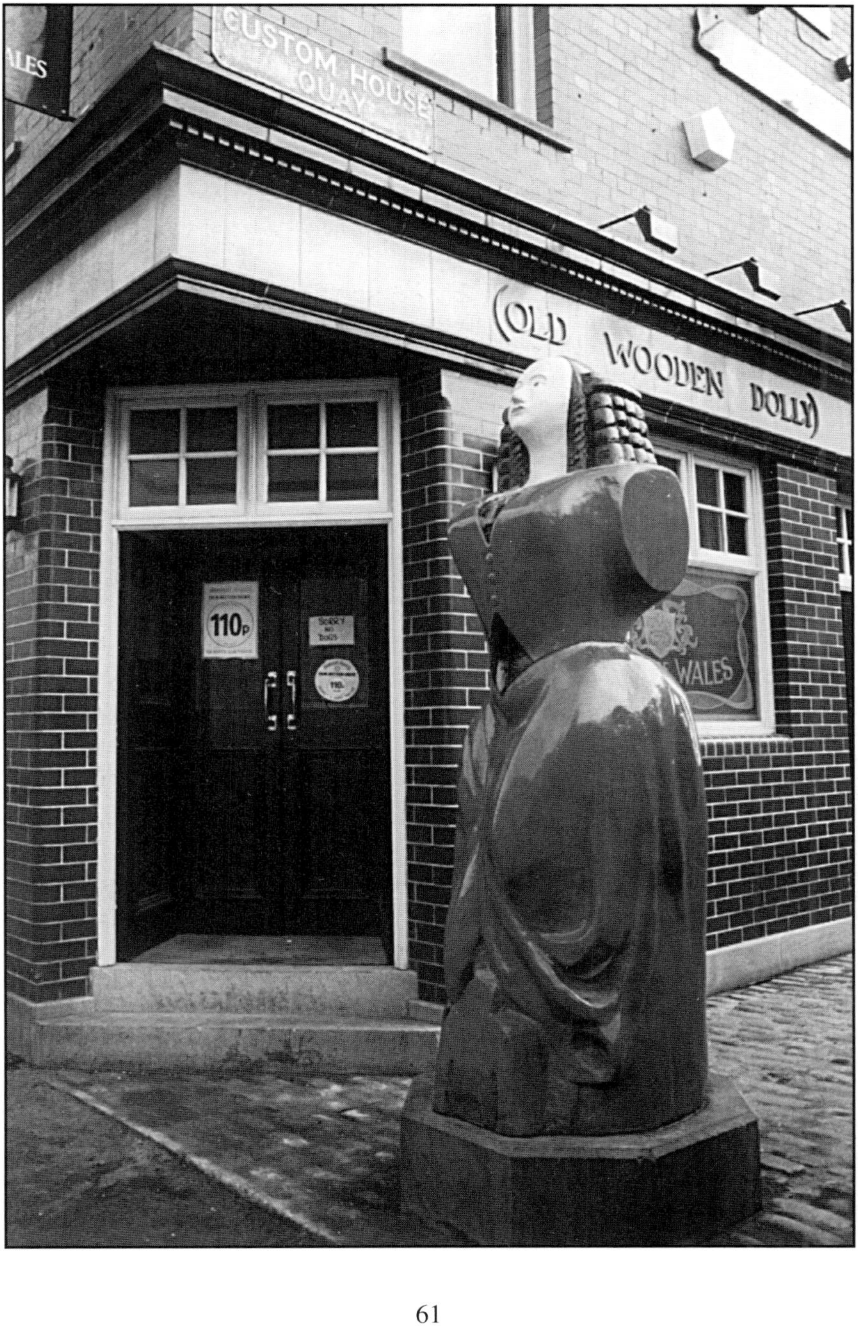
CUSTOM HOUSE
QUAY
(OLD WOODEN DOLLY)
110p

WOODEN DOLLY

"For many years she stood upon the Fish Quay
A problematic symbol of the past
The figurehead of some forgotten trader
She had travelled many miles before the mast.

And everyone paid homage to the lady
She was worshipped by the seamen's brotherhood
Amazing when you think that she was only
An ordinary Dolly made of wood."

Ripyard Cuddling